100 THINGS WILD FANS
SHOULD KNOW & DO
BEFORE THEY DIE

Dan Myers

30 YEARS

TRIUMPH
BOOKS

Library of Congress Cataloging-in-Publication Data

Names: Myers, Dan (Sportswriter), author.
Title: 100 things Wild fans should know & do before they die / Dan Myers.
Other titles: One hundred things Wild fans should know and do before they die
Description: Chicago, IL : Triumph Books, [2019] | Summary: "This books is about the history the Minnesota Wild franchise"— Provided by publisher.
Identifiers: LCCN 2019023197 | ISBN 9781629375120 (trade paperback)
Subjects: LCSH: Minnesota Wild (Hockey team)—History—Juvenile literature. | Hockey players—Juvenile literature. | Sports spectators—Juvenile literature.
Classification: LCC GV848.M58 M94 2019 | DDC 796.962/6409776579—dc23
LC record available at https://lccn.loc.gov/2019023197

This book is available in quantity at special discounts for your group or organization. For further information, contact:

Triumph Books LLC
814 North Franklin Street
Chicago, Illinois 60610
(312) 337-0747
www.triumphbooks.com

Printed in U.S.A.
ISBN: 978-1-62937-512-0
Design by Patricia Frey
Photos courtesy of AP Images unless otherwise indicated

To my dad…thanks for bringing me to my first hockey game, a spark that ignited a passion that burns today and for every day forward.

Contents

Foreword

I remember the night I fell in love with Minnesota.

I was playing for the Atlanta Thrashers at the time. It was late in the day on New Year's Day in 2001, and we had just lost to the Washington Capitals. We hopped on our team plane and headed west, where we were set to play the Wild a couple of days later.

Take a look out the window the next time you're descending into Minneapolis–St. Paul International Airport and you'll see exactly what I saw that night, a sight that made me believe this was a place I could one day envision myself playing hockey.

After spending my career playing in warmer climates like Nashville and Atlanta, what I saw that night will stick with me forever. A minute or two from landing, I looked out my window and saw what seemed like a scene out of a snow globe.

As far as I could see, there were frozen lakes and ponds and backyard rinks with floodlights lighting the night. Every sheet of ice had what seemed like 20 kids on it. As a kid from northern Ontario, it was a scene not unlike the ones I grew up with back in Sudbury.

A few minutes later, we got off the plane and walked down the steps. A light snow was falling.

In that moment, I remember thinking: *this feels like home.*

I didn't know it at the time, but my future was destined to bring me back here, first as a player (twice), then as a coach and an executive. In the months and years that followed, Minnesota no longer felt like home…it became home.

It didn't take me long to realize just how special this place truly is.

The day after we landed, we had some downtime in St. Paul. I went and grabbed a coffee, and people in the shop were talking about the Gophers. At dinner that night, folks at the next table were excited for the Wild game the following night and talking about high school hockey.

Hockey was everywhere.

Two nights later, I prepared to step on the Xcel Energy Center ice for the first time with expectations rather low. It was two days after New Year's, two expansion teams were getting ready to play a weeknight game, and undoubtedly there were other things going on that would take people away from the rink.

As we came out of the tunnel that night, I was blown away. The arena was packed, the energy was palpable, and you could feel the passion Wild fans had for their team and for this sport.

The following summer, I became an unrestricted free agent. I had spent six years in the NHL with three different teams. Unsure of how long I'd be in the league, I thought about the opportunity to join a team that could make a championship run. I thought about the potential of playing back in my home country of Canada. I thought about a lot of different things.

Then the Wild called, and I got to thinking about that New Year's night that would forever change my life. And in that moment, everything became clear.

I signed on in Minnesota and had some of the best seasons of my career. When the lockout canceled the 2004–05 season, I chose to stick around and take in as much of the hockey culture of the state as I could. I helped Larry Hendrickson coach a high school team. I broadcasted state tournament games.

I wanted to do everything I could to immerse myself in the Minnesota hockey community.

Following the lockout, I played three years in Colorado before once again having the chance to sign with the Wild.

It was a no-brainer. This was home.

When my playing career ended, I was lucky enough to stick around, working two seasons behind the bench as an assistant coach before transitioning to a front-office role that allowed me the chance to continue shaping the future of pro hockey in this incredible market.

Even though the ultimate goal of a Stanley Cup was not achieved, I do not regret a second of my time here.

—Andrew Brunette
Former Wild left wing
Former Wild assistant general manager

1 Becoming the Wild

When the National Hockey League decided to return to Minnesota in 1997, the city and the franchise had three years before it would ever see the ice.

Perhaps the most important piece of business to figure out during that time was what it would do about its nickname.

It had been four years since the North Stars left for Dallas, Texas, and though that franchise had dropped the "North" and became simply the "Stars" upon its arrival in the Lone Star State, many in Minnesota wanted the new franchise to harken back to its roots and secure its legendary old "N" logo. "People wanted that. [But] Dallas owned the rights to the name 'Stars' and all their history at that point, and people didn't really understand that," said Bill Robertson, the Wild's first vice president of communications and broadcasting. "They weren't going to relinquish it, so it couldn't happen. But there was an outpour of people who wanted that."

Owner Bob Naegele thought it was possible for a new NHL team in Minnesota to try and connect with its roots, but at the same time, start with a blank slate. So he had Jac Sperling, a minority owner and the team's vice chairman, go about finding one.

The team solicited fans for ideas on what they wanted to see, asking them to write letters with suggestions for a new nickname. Sperling took the job very seriously, according to Robertson. There was rarely a letter Sperling didn't open himself.

Eventually, the organization and its marketing firm narrowed down the list to six potential team names: the Wild, the Freeze, the Northern Lights, the Blue Ox, the Voyageurs, and the White Bears.

All six names had strong ties to Minnesota's famously chilly climate, and some had intriguing branding possibilities. But in the end, "Wild" was the one chosen.

Years later, the NHL took control of team names for franchises that relocated, including the North Stars, Nordiques, and the first reincarnation of the Winnipeg Jets, who moved to Phoenix in 1995. When the Atlanta Thrashers were purchased by True North Sports and Entertainment in 2011 and moved to Winnipeg, the Jets was the overwhelming favorite among fans as the choice for the team's new nickname.

It's likely Naegele and his group would have faced similar pressure from local fans had that option been available to them in the late 1990s. "I think it would have been considered heavily," Robertson said. "But I think there is another current of thought that we wanted to be something different than that. We don't want to have to be the exact same. The Cleveland Browns became the Cleveland Browns again, kind of in the same vein. But there was a thought of, 'It would be kind of cool to have that nostalgic piece and carry it on,' and others thought it might not be, it might be good to create our own identity."

2 Building from the Back

As Wild general manager Doug Risebrough entered the expansion draft process in 2000, he had one clear objective in mind: find a way to build his new team with speed and build it from the back forward. "The player pool was not nearly as good as the one Vegas had [in 2017]," Risebrough said, "which is just the way it should be. They spent a lot of money to get an expansion team; they deserved to get the players they got."

Once it became clear the Wild would select third in the 2000 Entry Draft, guaranteeing it would have the option to pick one of goaltender Rick DiPietro or forwards Dany Heatley and Marian Gaborik, Risebrough wanted the focus to be on his blue line in the expansion draft.

The Wild had already worked out a deal for goaltender Manny Fernandez, a player Risebrough was comfortable hailing as a top goaltender. Minnesota wanted to find someone to push Fernandez in the crease and players that could help keep his crease clean in front of him. "We knew we had one good goalie, and we were looking to get another good goalie," Risebrough said. "We really tried to focus on defensemen."

Because of the rules of the draft, wherein each existing franchise (minus Nashville and Atlanta) could only lose one defenseman and one goaltender in total, Minnesota and Columbus each focused on those areas early.

Minnesota had won the coin flip between the clubs and chose to pick higher in the entry draft, which meant Columbus selected first in the expansion draft. With that pick, the Blue Jackets chose goaltender Rick Tabaracci.

The Wild countered with two goaltenders of their own, Jamie McLennan and Mike Vernon, who would be traded to Calgary for forward Dan Cavanaugh and an eighth-round pick in the 2001 NHL Draft.

Columbus countered with two more goaltenders and two familiar names to Wild fans: Frederic Chabot, who would later go on to become the club's goaltending development coach, and Dwayne Roloson, who never played for the Blue Jackets and signed with the St. Louis Blues' minor league affiliate instead. Roloson would eventually sign with the Wild as a free agent the following summer and play parts of four seasons with the club.

The Wild finished up the run of goaltenders by selecting Chris Terreri, who it shipped back to New Jersey (the team from which he was plucked) along with a draft pick for defenseman Brad Bombardir.

But Bomber wasn't the first defenseman the Wild would end up with that day that made a difference.

The first non-goalie picked in the expansion draft was defenseman Sean O'Donnell, who played 63 games with Minnesota during its first season. It also picked Curtis Leschyshyn, who played in 54 contests. "[O'Donnell] was perfect for us because he was a big, strong even-tempered guy who had a physical presence," Risebrough said. "And he was proud of being the top defenseman with a lot of young guys. I remember thinking O'Donnell would be our guy, and if we could get him, that would be a good start."

Those two were the best known of its chosen blue liners at the time, but they didn't have the longest tenures with the club.

Ladislav Benysek spent parts of three years with the organization, playing in 145 games during the first two years of the Wild. With the 15th pick of the expansion draft, Minnesota selected little-known Filip Kuba from the Calgary Flames. "All unknowns. Nobody knew about Filip Kuba, nobody knew about Benysek," Risebrough said. "I often stuck to the idea of really wanting mobility, and both of those guys came on because of their mobility. Give them credit; they put in the work to become the players [they eventually became]. But the day they were drafted, not a lot of people knew them, and quite frankly, we didn't know them that well either."

Kuba, who had just 18 games of NHL experience in two prior seasons, would go on to play five seasons for Minnesota and make an NHL All-Star team in 2004. He still ranks as one of the best defensemen in team history, having scored 33 goals and 132 points in 357 games with the Wild. He finished his NHL career in 2013 having skated in 836 games in the league.

Minnesota hit on some of its forward picks later in the draft as well.

Scott Pellerin was plucked from the St. Louis Blues and scored 11 goals in his only season with the club. Jim Dowd played four seasons with the Wild after being selected 30th overall. With the 43rd pick, Minnesota chose Richfield, Minnesota, native Darby Hendrickson, who would go on to play four seasons with his hometown team and score the first goal in the first home game in franchise history.

3 Riser

Most any former Montreal Canadien boasts a Stanley Cup ring or two and a lofty winning percentage as a player. Doug Risebrough is no different.

In just his second season in the NHL in 1976, Risebrough was a part of a Stanley Cup winning team with the Canadiens, one that would go on to win four consecutive Cups before the end of the decade.

After a trade to the Calgary Flames in 1982, Risebrough became a respected captain and one who brought the Flames to the Stanley Cup Finals in 1986, only to lose to his old organization, the Canadiens.

Upon retiring, Risebrough moved behind the bench in Calgary, where he won the Stanley Cup in 1989 as an assistant coach. He moved into management the following year, serving as assistant general manager for one season and head coach for a year and a half while also becoming just the second GM in Calgary's history.

Risebrough maintained his GM spot in Calgary until November of 1995, then became vice president of hockey operations down the road with the Edmonton Oilers, a role he served in until 1999.

When the Minnesota Wild called about hiring him as its first-ever GM, Risebrough was indifferent. Edmonton had made the playoffs all three seasons he was with the organization, and he wasn't necessarily looking to move on.

Glen Sather, the GM of the Oilers at the time, got a call from the Wild asking for permission to speak to Risebrough, but Sather wouldn't sign off on it until after arbitration hearings were held in August. At that point, the Wild were only one year away from hitting the ice for its first training camp; Columbus, which entered the same year as Minnesota, had hired its GM months earlier in the process.

Risebrough was fine with holding off, though. "I wasn't really thinking of leaving, I liked the job I was doing," Risebrough said. "Then sure enough, I got a call from Jac Sperling, I met with him twice, I met with Bob [Naegele] once, and things went fast. The more I was there [in Minnesota], the more I realized I was ready to leave [Edmonton] too. You don't think about leaving until there is an opportunity, and I've always been a guy to do the job that's just in front of me, not architect where I'm gonna be. But when this opportunity was there, I thought it would be a good fit."

On September 2, 1999, Risebrough was named the Wild's first general manager. It was a unique opportunity for him to start completely from scratch and build a franchise from the ground up. "What people see are the players, and everybody is getting a chance where maybe they didn't get a chance before," Risebrough said. "But the whole staff is like that, the whole operation. The energy level behind an expansion team is just phenomenal. It's everywhere, everyone is having a good day all the time."

In searching for his first head coach, his list began and ended with one name: former Montreal teammate Jacques Lemaire.

An eight-time Stanley Cup champion as a player, twice more as an assistant GM with the Canadiens, and once more as head coach of the New Jersey Devils in 1995, Lemaire brought with him a resumé boasting one main trait: "He's a winner," Risebrough said.

Building a winning tradition was Risebrough's primary objective when he set about laying the foundation of the franchise. But how does one do that when you're building from scratch?

In Risebrough's eyes, it was about bringing in as many people with that shared background as possible. "I got winners there," Risebrough said. "[Former assistant coach] Mike Ramsey is a winner. Jacques is a winner. [Former assistant coach] Mario [Tremblay] was a winner. Darby Hendrickson is a winner. [Andrew] Brunette is a winner. [Sean] O'Donnell was a winner. I always say, I stole tradition and stole winning from a lot of different places."

Risebrough found building an expansion team to be far more gratifying than he thought the experience would be, mostly because he was able to retrain his mind to find a new comfort zone. "As an experienced GM, you always fear the unknown: this player is going to leave, and there is nothing you can do about it, or this coach is gonna retire; what are you gonna do about it? It drives you crazy," Risebrough said. "The biggest thing I learned in Minnesota as an expansion general manager was: it's *all* unknown. If you don't embrace unknown, you're not going to have fun, and it was way better than I thought."

4 The Minnesota Jets?

Had the original Winnipeg Jets secured their first choice of relocation, the Wild may not exist today.

Following the 1994–95 season, things were especially bleak for the Jets. Rising operating costs and bloated player salaries made things especially tough for the NHL's Canadian franchises. It was especially tough for Winnipeg, which was the league's smallest city after the Quebec Nordiques relocated to Denver in 1995 and became the Avalanche.

The Canadian dollar was also struggling and only worth around 70 cents American. The lockout during the 1994–95 season made things worse, costing the Jets and every other team half its home gate revenue.

Its home at the time, Winnipeg Arena, was nearly 40 years old. And despite the fact that local fans routinely packed the old barn, it held just 12,500 fans, 2,000 below the NHL average.

The Jets were nearly saved at the last moment by a group of Winnipeg businessmen, who had agreed to buy the franchise and build it a new arena. But when the deal fell through in April of 1995, the writing was on the wall.

The following month, Jets owner Barry Shenkarow agreed to sell the club for $68 million to a group led by Minneapolis businessman Richard Burke, who along with Steven Gluckstern, planned to move the team 300 miles southeast.

The Twin Cities had been without professional hockey for two seasons after the Minnesota North Stars bolted for Dallas. In the meantime, the Metropolitan Sports Center, the Bloomington home of the North Stars during their existence in Minnesota, had been demolished to make way for the Mall of America.

Burke was prepared to move the Jets to downtown Minneapolis and the five-year-old Target Center, home of the NBA's Minnesota Timberwolves. But state assistance was needed, in the form of $20 million from the state legislature.

Minnesota's politicians were prepared to talk with Burke in an effort to bring professional hockey back to Minnesota, but according to former Minnesota governor Arne Carlson, it was a one-way street. "Burke was extraordinarily difficult to work with. It was a constant refusal to examine his financials," said Carlson, a two-term Republican from Minneapolis who led the state from 1991–99. "We wanted to know who we were doing business with financially. And if we couldn't get the financials, we weren't going to do any kind of a deal. He was extremely silent, and I'm not sure whether the relationship just fizzled, or whether we just severed it. But either way, we were not going forward."

When Minnesota's politicians failed to provide the subsidy, the deal fell through once again allowing the people of Manitoba the chance to save its team. A grassroots campaign raised millions of dollars, and the once bleak future of the Jets in Winnipeg appeared to be on solid ground again.

But in August with tens of thousands of people in the streets of downtown Winnipeg, fans were told their efforts had come up short. The 1995–96 season would be its final campaign in southern Manitoba, as the team was indeed being sold to Burke and Gluckstern—this time with the intent of moving the team to Phoenix. In December, the agreement was finalized and hockey in the desert became official: the Phoenix Coyotes were born.

Two years later, the NHL announced Minnesota would receive an expansion franchise, thanks to a joint effort between the state of Minnesota, the city of St. Paul, and businessman Bob Naegele.

The experience this time around couldn't have been more different. "I don't think the process itself, at least the process of getting a team, I don't think it ever stopped [after the potential move of the Jets fell through]. I don't recall how many different leads we had, but there were several," Carlson said. "Obviously, the one that ultimately panned out was when Bob Naegele stepped forth, and he was a perfect delight to work with."

Jacques Lemaire

After the Wild hired Doug Risebrough as its first general manager in 1999, the next thing on the franchise's checklist was to hire a head coach to supervise the on-ice product on a day-to-day basis.

There were a number of different paths the Wild could have taken in hiring the position, but in wanting to establish a winning culture early, Risebrough's first call was to his old Montreal Canadiens teammate and former New Jersey Devils coach, Jacques Lemaire.

One of the greatest players in NHL history, Lemaire was a part of eight Stanley Cup championship teams with the Canadiens. As a coach, he led the Devils to the championship in 1995 and helped New Jersey to the playoffs in five of his seven seasons there.

Few in the history of the game had engineered a more impressive winning resumé than Lemaire, who had been out of coaching since leaving the Devils following the 1997–98 season.

Getting Lemaire wasn't going to be as simple as flying to Florida—his home since leaving the NHL—and presenting him with a boatload of cash. Risebrough would have to recruit the coach and provide the right opportunity.

Fortunately for Risebrough, he was presenting the exact kind of opportunity that Lemaire craved. So the new GM made a couple of trips to Florida, and the interest on Lemaire's part continued to increase. Once it became apparent that he'd be the first coach of the Wild, Risebrough remembered asking an important question. "We talked a lot about the process. And I remember asking him why he wanted the job," Risebrough recalled. "He said to me, 'It's the ultimate coaching job. Everybody will need coaching.'"

Talk to any former player about Lemaire, especially those that played for him during his tenure in Minnesota, and to a man, they'll rave about Lemaire's ability to teach. With a roster void of proven superstars and a blank slate with which to work, Lemaire had the opportunity to be the teacher he so desired with the Wild. "He was the automatic choice because he had experience. He had

Jacques Lemaire directs his Wild team during a first-round playoff series in 2008.

a winning tradition. I knew he would bring a winning attitude for our players," Risebrough said. "And he's arguably the brightest coach I've ever worked with. His ability to work with players and make them better was outstanding. And he really wanted to do the job."

When Lemaire was introduced as the team's first coach on June 19, 2000, he preached patience, something he would have to remind himself of on many occasions. "I know that I will have to be patient, the fans will have to be patient, but I'm telling you, we're going to win our share of games," Lemaire said that day. Few could have expected how correct the coach would be in his assessment. By year three, Lemaire led the Wild to the Western Conference Finals, the franchise's furthest foray into the Stanley Cup Playoffs.

Lemaire would remain behind the Wild bench for the club's first eight seasons, guiding the team to its only division championship in 2008 and three berths in the postseason.

In 656 games, Lemaire posted a 293–255–55–53 record as coach, a winning percentage of 53 percent. Lemaire was right; it would win its fair share of games. It would win more than it lost during his tenure.

6 Bob Naegele

With the potential of the NHL's return to Minnesota slipping away, Bob Naegele Jr. stepped up and grabbed the opportunity to be the man to make it happen.

A number of local business leaders and potential investors met at the Town and Country Club in St. Paul to discuss bringing professional hockey back to Minnesota four years after the North Stars had left for Dallas.

All were interested in ownership of a new team, but it seemed none were willing to take the lead. "We've got all these people who say they are interested [in ownership], someone needs to take the lead. Nobody did anything," said Bill Robertson, the Wild's first vice president of communications and broadcasting. "And Bob, something went off in his mind, and he said, 'I'm going to take the lead.'"

A few months later, he sat on the stage with a folded copy of *Let's Play Hockey* magazine, which he unfurled and said with a huge smile, "Hockey's back!"

While Naegele took the lead in getting the team to St. Paul, he was extremely hands off once it was. His goal was to find and hire the very best people for every job, then trust them to be great leaders.

Naegele wanted his own team to take ownership of every aspect of the Wild, even before it was called that. Robertson explained it this way: "Part of his talk with me coming back to the Wild was, 'We want you here because part of your legacy will be that you helped return the NHL to Minnesota.' That's a powerful message to be able to say as one of the founding employees of the organization," Robertson said. "It was a cold night in December when I came back to visit with him. I was with the [Anaheim] Ducks at the time, and it was 80 degrees when I left. I wasn't sure that [coming back to St. Paul was] what I wanted to do. But when he and Jac [Sperling] put it like that to me in that powerful of a message, 'You're gonna be able to do a lot here,' I had to come back."

Pro hockey in Minnesota is a no-brainer now, but back in the mid-1990s, it was no sure thing. The North Stars were gone, and there was no clear building ready to take on a new tenant. The Met Center had been razed and, even if it hadn't, it was no longer fit for an NHL team.

Minneapolis' Target Center was brand new but wasn't ideal for hockey. It was also serving as the home of the NBA's Minnesota Timberwolves.

As eyes began turning to the other Twin City, St. Paul, many were skeptical. Pro sports in the city hadn't worked out in the past, specifically pro hockey. The Minnesota Fighting Saints and the Minnesota Moose had failed in the decades prior. What would make it different this time around?

With mayor Norm Coleman and others as partners, Naegele went about building the finest arena in the NHL and providing a one-of-a-kind fan experience that kept customers coming back.

The constant stream of doubters also kept him hungry. "I've always enjoyed when somebody says, 'You can't do that.' It's always proved to me to be a challenge," Naegele said. "When the North Stars left, I realized what a hole it left in the heart of everyone in Minnesota, whether you're a hockey fan or not. I had the opportunity—I was in the rare place and time—to change history. That became a primary motivator for me to take a swing at the puck. And now I see that fulfilled with the great success it's been."

Xcel Energy Center is one arena still trying to be replicated in cities around the country. It's been standing for nearly two decades, but still looks brand new, even to those that frequent it. "Others have tried to imitate it," Naegele said. "Yet it doesn't have the heart of the State of Hockey. They're just buildings that are built to imitate ours. But ours has that soul, and when you see it...I was walking through the lower level, and it's the cleanest building of any arena in the league. It's a pride for every employee that works for the Wild."

How many owners have you seen standing inside an arena or a stadium, greeting fans? You could find Naegele in the concourse inside Xcel Energy Center's Gate 1 nightly.

It was that kind of customer service that had the Wild rated as one of the best game-night experiences in all of sports for more than a decade. But it wasn't just paying customers that Naegele spent time with. It was his employees as well. "After just one meeting, whether you were an intern, or a director, he knew your name and took the time to say hi to you and ask how you were doing," said Wild director of public relations Aaron Sickman, one of Robertson's first hires before the team even took the ice. "He was a great person to work for and Wild fans couldn't have asked for a better person to bring the NHL back to Minnesota."

For his contributions to bringing professional hockey back to the state, the team awarded Naegele with its State of Hockey Legacy Award in March of 2018. It's a legacy Naegele carefully crafted and one he was certainly proud of. "It's important to have a good legacy, and what you do at the beginning effects the outcome," Naegele said. "To see the legacy that's here, I'm proud of it, and I'm proud of everybody that's been a part of it. It's such a blessing to hear about it. I believe we sowed good seeds, and they continue to grow up and become a good harvest. I'm out of the picture, yet the tradition carries on.

"It's so fun to see. None of us could have envisioned what the outcome would be 21 years later. We're all so excited about the rejuvenation of St. Paul and what the arena has done for the status of, not only of the city, but of the state of Minnesota."

Naegele passed away due to complications of cancer on November 7, 2018. The Wild honored him with a moment of silence prior to their next home game on November 13 and wore a patch with the initials "BN" on their jerseys for the remainder of the 2018–19 season.

7 Brunette's OT Goal in Colorado

A little more than three minutes into overtime of Game 7 against the Colorado Avalanche in the first round of the 2003 Stanley Cup Playoffs, the Wild's season had already lasted longer than anyone could have expected.

While the Wild entered the postseason as the sixth seed in the Western Conference, the Avalanche had a bevy of future Hall of Famers on their roster: Joe Sakic, Peter Forsberg, and Patrick Roy among them.

After getting through the end of regulation tied 2–2, the Pepsi Center in Denver seemed uneasy. Colorado, which was supposed to have an easy go in the first round, was being taken to the limit—and beyond—by a third-year franchise, whose best player was barely 21 years old.

Just 24 hours earlier and some 900 miles away in St. Paul, the Avalanche had the Wild against the ropes. After a scoreless first 40 minutes in Game 6, the Wild jumped out to a two-goal lead in the third on goals by Richard Park and Marian Gaborik. With four minutes left in regulation, Minnesota appeared primed to coast into Game 7 the following night in Colorado.

But Sakic's goal with 3:26 left got the Avs on the board, and when Greg de Vries followed with the tying salvo less than two minutes later, the young and inexperienced Wild appeared outgunned.

Park, however, made sure the Wild got its Game 7, when he slipped a shot through Roy's five hole 4:22 into the extra session, sending Xcel Energy Center into a frenzy.

Park's heroics were the talk of the town for about 24 hours.

Colorado led twice in Game 7, with Forsberg opening the scoring at 6:16 of the second period. Pascal Dupuis tied the game for the Wild less than two minutes later.

In the third, Sakic made it 2–1 on a power play goal with less than seven minutes remaining. But Gaborik countered with a power play goal of his own two minutes, 17 seconds after that.

In overtime Colorado made its final push. Wild goaltender Manny Fernandez had already seen 45 shots on goal, stopping 43 of them to keep the game knotted. "If that overtime was three minutes old, it was spent entirely in our defensive zone," said former Wild forward Wes Walz. "But we only needed one chance."

When Andrew Brunette and Sergei Zholtok exited the Avalanche zone two-on-two, things seemed inauspicious enough. One Wild player even peeled off for a quick line change as Minnesota worked the puck through neutral.

Things changed quickly as Zholtok continued to work the puck up ice, unimpeded. Just before splitting Avs' defensemen de Vries and Derek Morris, Zholtok dropped the puck straight back to Brunette.

In what can only be a massive miscommunication, de Vries (to Zholtok's left) and Morris (to his right), crisscrossed attempting to slow the Wild rush. As Zholtok's drop pass found Brunette, the veteran forward read the play beautifully, stepping to left and turning on what limited jets he had. De Vries slowed Morris down just enough for Brunette to get half a step on him. The lefty shot also had leverage, working around Morris. Because he was on his forehand, Roy had to respect the shot, committing early to cut down the angle. Brunette saw this as well, patiently pulling the puck to his backhand and slipping it inches past Roy's outstretched left leg pad for the winning goal.

The lasting image of Brunette's goal, which has almost entirely overshadowed Park's iconic moment the night before, is the bookend on Roy's career; the goaltender never played again and didn't resurface in the league until 2013, when he became head coach of the Avalanche.

More than 15 years since it happened, Brunette's goal remains as perhaps the high-water mark for an organization and a state still looking for its first-ever Stanley Cup championship.

8 Laying the Groundwork for Parise and Suter

July 1 is one of the few dates NHL fans circle on their summer calendars. While the Stanley Cup Finals have been over for two or three weeks and the NHL Draft is in the rearview mirror, the free agent frenzy that takes place on Canada Day is the final gathering spot for fans before a two-month slumber at training camp.

While teams have gotten pretty good at locking up their best players before July 1, the summer of 2012 dawned with two of the NHL's best players set to reach unrestricted free agency: forward Zach Parise of the New Jersey Devils and defenseman Ryan Suter of the Nashville Predators.

Parise, the son of former Minnesota North Star J.P. Parise and a native of Minneapolis, had just led the Devils to the Stanley Cup Finals, losing in six to the Los Angeles Kings.

Suter, the son of 1980 Olympic legend Bob Suter and a former Wisconsin Badger, was the left half of arguably the best defensive pairing in the NHL. Shea Weber was himself a restricted free agent, and while Nashville was interested in keeping both of its franchise blue liners, it wouldn't be an easy task.

While Parise had roots—and a summer home—in the Twin Cities, Suter's wife, Becky, grew up in nearby Bloomington. He craved the opportunity to play games closer to his family in

Madison, Wisconsin, just a four-hour drive from Xcel Energy Center on Interstate 94.

Still, it was rare for these kinds of players to each cast their lot with a mid-market franchise, roots or otherwise.

But don't think Wild general manager Chuck Fletcher wasn't willing to try. Fletcher, who was named the head of the club's hockey operations department in 2009, saw the summer of 2012 coming. He also assumed leadership of a system bare of high-end prospects and a salary cap bloated with players not worthy of their numbers. Beginning in 2010, Fletcher went about making moves with 2012 in mind, trading away bad contracts in exchange for other bad contracts…but at least these ones were shorter in length.

He traded away the team's best player, defenseman Brent Burns, for a haul of young players that included forward Devin Setoguchi and the rights to forward Charlie Coyle. He drafted Mikael Granlund, then selected Jonas Brodin in the first round in consecutive years. He made a bold play to trade up and get Jason Zucker in the second round. He picked Erik Haula in the seventh round.

Although clearing out the salary cap space for Parise and Suter was job No. 1, a close second was building a farm system worthy of attracting those veteran players, providing them with a dynamic supporting group that would allow the Wild to be competitive for years to come.

Others that would eventually compete with the Wild for their services had a bunch more equity.

The Detroit Red Wings are one of the most storied franchises in NHL history and had just come off a decade in which they won two Stanley Cups and lost another in seven games.

The Philadelphia Flyers were building their own Cup-worthy team, having lost in the finals to the Blackhawks just two years prior.

Minnesota offered the opportunity to come home…but what else? One division title in 11 years as a franchise? One extended—albeit magical—run to the Western Conference Finals a decade earlier?

Those other teams were also reportedly willing to offer much more money. What they couldn't offer Parise and Suter—longtime rivals at almost every level growing up—was an opportunity to play together.

In the end, it was one of the major reasons why the duo chose to bring their talents to Minnesota.

9 Fourth of July Game Changer

It was an unusually hot day, even for a fourth of July in Minnesota.

With the sun shining and people off work for the holiday, getting to a lake or finding a spot to celebrate the day was a priority, while hockey couldn't have been further from the minds of most.

At least early in the day.

It was 2012, and three months prior, the Wild had finished a season in which it was the best team in the league around Christmastime yet faltered so badly during the second half it missed the playoffs by 14 points. It was a stunning fall from grace even for a team that clearly played over its head for the first two months of the 2011–12 campaign.

But things were about to get a whole lot better.

The Wild were in the mix for two of the best free agents to ever reach the open market, local boy Zach Parise and defenseman Ryan Suter, and Minnesota had salary cap space to burn after a series of moves by general manager Chuck Fletcher in the years leading up

New Wild players Ryan Suter, left, and Zach Parise are introduced to the media on July 9, 2012.

to this summer. His hope: close on one of these marquee free agents to help rebuild the next era of Wild hockey.

The club had a number of quality young players about to reach the NHL; Mikael Granlund, Charlie Coyle, Jason Zucker, and Jonas Brodin were among the top prospects in the game, and Minnesota's farm system was viewed by many experts as the best.

Adding a player with the name value of a Parise or a Suter would be the cherry on top.

A little after noon, official word came down. The Wild weren't getting Parise *or* Suter. It was getting Parise *and* Suter. With the news, an entire franchise's fortunes changed in a matter of minutes.

The Wild sold out the first 409 consecutive preseason and regular season games in franchise history, a stretch that lasted nearly a decade. When it ended, it was the third-longest sellout streak in NHL history.

But by the time Mike Yeo took over as head coach in 2011, Xcel Energy Center was no longer filled to capacity. While the arena was still considered one of the best in the league, 10 years had gone by with only one extended playoff run and one division title.

Parise and Suter changed all of that. The Wild's once lengthy season-ticket waiting list, which had dwindled in the season before the signings, was full again. Attendance records were falling again. Another sellout streak began shortly thereafter.

Most importantly, the Wild were having their best success on the ice. Minnesota made the NHL playoffs in each of the first six seasons after signing Parise and Suter, a stretch matched by just two other teams in the league.

10 How Koivu Became Captain

It took the Wild eight seasons to name its first permanent captain.

Eight years and eight games to be exact.

Fortunately for the Wild, it's a job a coach has only had to do one time in the history of the franchise.

When Mikko Koivu was handed the C on a permanent basis in October of 2009, he became the first full-time captain in team history. Throughout the entire tenure of coach Jacques Lemaire, the captaincy was something the veteran coach used as a carrot to get his players to perform.

In the early years of the franchise, the team didn't have a veteran superstar to build around. For the most part, other than

Marian Gaborik, Lemaire's teams featured blue-collar, hard-working players that had been cast aside by at least one—and in some cases several—former teams. The rotating C was a way for Lemaire to put all of those players on an equal playing field.

Drafted sixth overall by the Wild in the 2001 draft, the Finnish born centerman didn't arrive in North America until 2004. But a lockout that canceled an entire NHL season robbed him of a chance to make the Wild in his first season in Minnesota, so he played an entire year for the club's AHL team in Houston.

As a rookie in 2005–06, Koivu was a bit underwhelming. A knee injury delayed the start of his career, but in 64 games, Koivu posted just six goals and 21 points.

It didn't take long for him to improve on those statistics.

He scored 20 goals and 54 points in his second season and added a second 20-goal season to go with 67 points by his fourth year, Lemaire's final one as coach of the Wild, in 2008–09.

The team made wholesale changes following that season, going in a different direction behind the bench while also firing general manager Doug Risebrough and hiring Chuck Fletcher.

It didn't take new head coach Todd Richards long to figure out he had captain material in Koivu. In a dressing room with vets like Owen Nolan and Andrew Brunette, Koivu—at the age of 26—was wise beyond his years. "Before I said yes, I asked them if it was all right with the veteran players on the team," Koivu wrote in *The Players' Tribune* in 2017. "That was something that was very important to me; I wanted to make sure the entire organization trusted me, including our players. The coaches told me they had spoken to our team, and that everyone was on board. They were behind it, and after that, I felt confident. That was the biggest thing for me to feel that they were behind me and supporting."

Koivu was a captain four times the year prior under Lemaire's monthly system, and the writing was on the wall even then. "Mikko possesses all the qualities you want your leader to have," Richards said upon naming Koivu captain on October 20, 2009. "He is passionate, has a great work ethic, and competes for everything. The way Mikko plays defines him as the leader of our team."

Since sewing the letter on his jersey a decade ago, the Wild hasn't had to remove or replace it. Koivu has signed a pair of contract extensions in Minnesota and is the franchise's all-time leader in virtually every statistic.

On Opening Night in 2000, the Wild retired the jersey No. 1 in honor of its fans. It seems almost certain that Koivu's No. 9 will one day join it as a number that will never be worn again. "This is my home. It's a very special place to me," Koivu wrote. "Being the captain of the Minnesota Wild has been one of the greatest honors of my life."

11 Nate Prosser

You know the old adage about cats having nine lives? That's sort of what Nate Prosser's career has been like with the Wild.

An Elk River, Minnesota, boy who played hockey at Colorado College, Prosser is the definition of a late bloomer. Never the best player on his team—at any level—Prosser was the little kid that always followed around his older brothers.

Once his career at Elk River High School was over, Prosser played three seasons of junior hockey before enrolling at CC as a 20-year-old freshman. Undrafted, he played in 137 games over four seasons. A solid senior season kept the door open for him to play professionally, and shortly after his final season in Colorado Springs, Prosser signed his first contract with his hometown Wild.

After making his NHL debut late in the 2009–10 season, Prosser played 73 games the following season with the team's AHL affiliate in Houston for first-year head coach Mike Yeo.

In 2011–12, Yeo moved to Minnesota. Prosser got his biggest opportunity yet, playing in 51 games with the Wild that season.

He's managed to somehow hang on the fringes of the National Hockey League ever since.

He played in 17 games in 2012–13 and 53 more in 2013–14.

The following summer, the Wild chose not to re-sign Prosser, who instead inked a two-way contract with the St. Louis Blues.

Apparently, the Wild realized their mistake quickly.

Prosser was waived by the Blues in training camp that fall… only to be claimed by Minnesota, where he played in a career high 63 games that season.

The right-handed defenseman played two more years in Minnesota before a weird bit of history repeated itself.

No longer wanted by the Wild, Prosser signed a two-year, two-way contract with the Blues again in the summer of 2017. St. Louis' head coach at the time? Yeo. "I had the inside knowledge of knowing his personality and what he'd do for our group," Yeo said. "A lot of the intangibles that we loved about him…there's so many intangibles that don't just show up on a scoresheet or are hard to measure with analytics. Certain players have the ability to make their teammates better and drag people into the fight, and he's one of those guys."

This time injuries kept Prosser in Missouri—for one game at least. Prosser played his first NHL game not in a Wild uniform on October 25, 2017, when the Blues hosted the Calgary Flames.

For the next month, Prosser was healthy scratched. As injured players continued to filter back into the lineup for St. Louis, Prosser was waived by the Blues yet again.

Waiting to pounce? Once again, his hometown Wild. "I just talked to a lot of the St. Louis guys about that, how bizarre this

NHL can be. I can be a No. 8 in St. Louis and come here and be an every day guy," Prosser said. "It's a very bizarre situation."

Prosser was just what the club needed: a right-shot blueliner and an injection of dressing room penicillin. "I'm sure every team quite frankly has one of those guys, and he's it for us," said Wild coach Bruce Boudreau. "He's not overly fast, doesn't have a great shot…But you add it all together, he's a good team guy that will do what it takes to win games. And that's why we liked him."

12 Minnesota Returns to the Ice

After three years of hype, the construction of a state-of-the-art arena, and a preseason of hockey, the Wild officially returned to the ice on October 6, 2000, when it played the Mighty Ducks at Arrowhead Pond in Anaheim, California.

After a scoreless first period, the Mighty Ducks scored 3:07 into the second on a goal by Jim Cummins. The lone assist on the goal was from Dan Bylsma, who would go on to become a successful head coach in the NHL.

Just over 12 minutes later, it was one of their own—future Wild forward Matt Cullen—a Moorhead, Minnesota, native and St. Cloud State alum, making it 2–0 on a power play goal.

With 1:01 left in the second Marian Gaborik scored the first goal in franchise history, pulling the Wild to within one goal after two periods. Scott Pellerin and Jim Dowd tallied assists on the goal.

Minnesota remained within striking distance for a chunk of the third period before Marty McInnis made it 3–1 with just more than 11 minutes left in regulation. Mike Leclerc assisted on each of Anaheim's final two goals.

The Wild wouldn't get any closer, as goaltender Jamie "Noodles" McLennan made 36 saves in a losing effort. Guy Hebert was stellar on the other side, making 35 saves in the victory.

For the Wild the game was about missed opportunity.

After killing an early Matt Johnson penalty, the Wild had a two-minute, five-on-three power play after Niclas Havelid (slashing) and Ladislav Kohn (elbowing) were each tagged for penalties 11:30 into the contest.

Minnesota wasn't able to capitalize but got another power play chance later in the first when Andrei Nazarov was taken to the box for holding the stick at the 17-minute mark. Ladislav Benysek committed an interference minor 67 seconds into the power play, however, ending the Wild's string of chances.

Even after Cummins' goal gave the Ducks the lead, Minnesota had two more power plays to try and tie it. Jason Marshall and Ruslan Salei took penalties, giving the Wild almost four minutes of consecutive power plays midway through the second period, but again came up empty.

Sure enough, Minnesota's Curtis Leschyshyn took a roughing penalty late in the second, and Cullen cashed in just over a minute into the man advantage, stretching the Ducks' lead to two.

The Wild would need to wait a bit before finding its first win in the NHL.

The following night in Arizona, Minnesota lost 4–1 to the Phoenix Coyotes to fall to 0–2.

The Wild opened Xcel Energy Center on October 11 with a 3–3 tie against the Philadelphia Flyers, earning the first point in franchise history. Fittingly, it was Richfield, Minnesota, native Darby Hendrickson scoring the first goal for the Wild that night. Jeff Nielsen, from Grand Rapids, Minnesota, assisted on Wes Walz's short-handed tally midway through the third period, which gave the Wild a brief 3–2 lead.

But Eric Desjardins tied the game just over a minute later, and the teams would skate even the rest of the way.

Two more losses followed, to St. Louis and to Edmonton, before Minnesota would find the win column for the first time on October 18 against the Tampa Bay Lightning.

13 A Run for the Record Books

As the 2002–03 regular season wound down, the expansion Wild secured its first-ever spot in the Stanley Cup Playoffs.

Just reaching the postseason was an accomplishment; Minnesota was in its third year of existence and had yet to spend big money on a free agent or trade for a big-name player.

But thanks to the efforts of a number of under-the-radar players who played their specific roles to a T, as well as the system put in place by then coach Jacques Lemaire, the Wild were finishing sixth in the Western Conference race with 42 wins and 95 points.

Unfortunately for the Wild, its playoff run wasn't expected to go very far. In the first round, Minnesota was set to face the Northwest Division champion Colorado Avalanche, a team that had several future Hall of Famers, including forwards Joe Sakic and Peter Forsberg, defenseman Rob Blake, and goaltender Patrick Roy.

Colorado won three of the first four games of the series, taking a commanding—but completely expected—lead in the series. The Wild won the first game of the series in Denver but watched the Avs win the next three, including both games at Xcel Energy Center, where the Wild scored only one goal on home ice.

Minnesota would win the next three games, however, all by the same 3–2 margin.

Game 5 in Denver marked the Wild's second win in three games at the Pepsi Center, sending the game back to St. Paul for the first of consecutive overtime winners. Richard Park scored first in Game 6 before Andrew Brunette's legendary winner in Game 7 capped the incredible comeback. Brunette's goal to wrap up the series was the final moment of Roy's career; the legendary goaltender retired after the season.

In round two, the Wild were once again the underdogs as they took on the fourth-seeded Vancouver Canucks.

Just three days after dispatching the Avalanche, the Wild were back in action on the road, this time at General Motors Place in Vancouver.

Once again, the game went to overtime but this time under much different circumstances. A pair of third-period goals by Wes Walz gave the Wild a 3–1 lead with under nine minutes to play in regulation. Markus Naslund got Vancouver within a goal at 11:12 of the third before Matt Cooke's goal with just 1.2 seconds remaining sent the game to the extra session. There, Minnesota native Trent Klatt won it for the Canucks on a goal 3:42 in, giving the favorites the 1–0 lead in the series.

Klatt's goal easily could have been a soul-crusher for the upstart Wild, but Minnesota responded with a 3–2 win in Game 2, holding onto a 3–1 lead in the third period and surviving yet another comeback attempt by Vancouver late in the contest.

Back in St. Paul, the Wild dropped a pair of 3–2 games, including one in overtime of Game 4, falling behind 3–1 in the series for a second consecutive round.

Yet again, the Wild came roaring back. Minnesota scored five times in the second period of Game 5—including two goals from Cliff Ronning—in a 7–2 win at GM Place. The Wild kept the offensive attack going back on home ice, as a pair of Brunette goals bookended a 5–1 win at Xcel Energy Center.

Facing do-or-die on the road, Minnesota fell behind 2–0 in Game 7, as Vancouver scored both goals just one minute apart midway through the game. Pascal Dupuis got one of the goals back three minutes after Todd Bertuzzi gave the home team a two-goal lead, pulling the Wild to within one with 20 minutes left.

As he had all series, Walz came up big, scoring the tying goal 8:05 into the third before Minnesota's own Darby Hendrickson—a former Vancouver Canuck—scored what would eventually be the game-winning goal at 14:48.

A late Dupuis goal with the man advantage iced things, as Minnesota became the first team in NHL history—and to date the only team—to overcome two 3–1 series deficits in the same postseason.

Facing seventh-seeded Anaheim in the Western Conference Finals, the Wild had home-ice advantage for the first time and went toe-to-toe with the Mighty Ducks in a scoreless Game 1 in St. Paul.

The Wild outshot Anaheim 39–26 but could not find a way to beat goaltender Jean-Sebastien Giguere, whose epic paddle save on Marian Gaborik with just under nine minutes to play in the second period kept the game at 0–0.

It's a play that still haunts Wild fans; would Minnesota have won the game in regulation? And how would that have changed the fortunes of that series?

Giguere would go on to post shutouts in Games 2 and 3 of the series as well, a stretch of nearly 218 minutes, surrendering his first—and only—goal of the series to Brunette four minutes into Game 4 at the Arrowhead Pond in Anaheim. Adam Oates scored a pair of goals later in the game, however, which was more than enough for Giguere, who made 24 saves to finish off the series sweep.

Anaheim would lose in the Stanley Cup Finals to the New Jersey Devils, but Giguere won the Conn Smythe Trophy as the Most Valuable Player of the postseason, the most recent of just five players in NHL history to win the award without hoisting Lord Stanley's cup.

14 Marian Gaborik

The Wild were certain it wanted one of three players from the 2000 NHL Draft. However, there was a 50 percent chance it would come away with the fourth pick overall and get none of the projected trio at the top.

Draft weekend in Calgary was going to be a busy one. First, the Wild and Columbus Blue Jackets would partake in an expansion draft, filling their rosters with a number of cast-offs from other organizations around the league.

The following day, the NHL would begin its traditional selection meeting with the New York Islanders and Atlanta Thrashers assured the top two picks in the draft.

Either the Wild or Blue Jackets would pick third, depending on the result of a coin toss prior to the expansion draft. The winner of the flip would decide: third pick in the entry draft or first pick in the expansion.

Desperately wanting one of the three consensus players at the top of the entry draft, Minnesota needed to win the coin toss. It did, and general manager Doug Risebrough quickly chose the third pick in the entry. Now it was simply a matter of which of the three players would fall to the Wild: goaltender Rick DiPietro, forward Dany Heatley, or forward Marian Gaborik.

After that, there was a significant drop off in talent. Rostislav Klesla, Raffi Torres, and Scott Hartnell would end up being the next three players off the board, but the trio of DiPietro, Heatley, and Gaborik had the potential to be game changers—or in the case of the Wild, a franchise cornerstone. "It was pretty well unanimous among our staff that there were three top players there," Risebrough said.

Perhaps it's lip service, but now nearly two decades after the selection was made, Risebrough insists Gaborik was the No. 1 player on the Wild's draft board, meaning the events of that day worked out perfectly for Minnesota; DiPietro was picked first by the Islanders while Heatley went second to the Thrashers, leaving the Wild to get its man. "We didn't know at that time who we were going to take, but we knew we would get one of the three," Risebrough said. "And it turned out, we ended up getting him."

While DiPietro and Heatley would go on to be NHL All-Stars, none would have the staying power of Gaborik, who surpassed the 1,000-game plateau in the league during the 2017–18 season.

Back in 2000, the Wild were enthralled with his speed and quick shot, skills that would serve him well in a career spanning nearly two decades in the NHL. "Ridiculous, explosive speed," said longtime former Wild teammate and line mate Wes Walz. "His first four strides were more powerful than any other player I'd seen at that time as an 18-year-old kid."

Risebrough wanted to draft someone the fans in Minnesota would rise to their feet to watch, and for eight seasons, Gaborik did just that. On a team filled mostly with career journeymen, Gaborik—especially early in his career—had the uncanny ability to make an entire arena hold its breath as he entered the offensive zone off the rush.

Most nights, he was the best player on the ice, and everyone—especially in the Wild dressing room—knew it. "We really cared about him," Walz said. "We knew we were going to be out of

Marian Gaborik, the first Wild player in franchise history to be named an All-Star, picks up the puck during the third period of a home game against the Vancouver Canucks in 2003.

the league, and he was going to be a superstar. We tried our best to nurture him and bring him along. There were times when he wanted to get outside the circle because he was so much better than all of us. But when one of us grabbed him by the collar, he'd never fight. He always came back. He bought in, and we were lucky to have him."

In eight years with the Wild, Gaborik never played in a full 82-game season, as injuries or holdouts limited his full potential to do even more damage to the Wild record book. Perhaps it's no coincidence that his only season of 80-plus games came in 2002–03, Minnesota's best season in franchise history. In 81 games Gaborik scored 30 goals and reached 65 points for the second straight year.

He would have better statistical seasons for certain—he scored a franchise-record 42 goals and 83 points in 77 games in 2007–08—but having Gaborik in the lineup every night made the Wild a better team.

Gaborik set a Wild record by scoring five goals in a single game on December 20, 2007, against Henrik Lundqvist and the New York Rangers. He remains the only player in franchise history to accomplish the feat.

After that season with unrestricted free agency just one year away, the Wild offered Gaborik a deal that went seven years and would have reportedly paid him more than $8 million per season.

Gaborik rejected the offer and played in just 17 games in an injury-marred final season with the Wild, scoring 13 goals and 23 points in what was his best points-per-game season of his tenure with the club.

Because of the injuries, the Wild were unable to get something in return for Gaborik, who eventually signed as a free agent with the New York Rangers. Gaborik felt constrained by Lemaire's defense-first system for years, and Risebrough and Gaborik's agent, Ron Salcer, were also on the outs after years of contentious contract negotiations.

The departures of both Lemaire and Risebrough earlier that summer had little effect on Gaborik, who seemed destined to begin anew somewhere else. He would do just that with the Rangers, where he spent the next three and a half years of his career, twice scoring 40-plus goals.

He would also go on to play for Columbus, the Los Angeles Kings, and the Ottawa Senators.

15 Watch a Game in Chicago

Fans looking for more of a traditional hockey experience can head to Chicago, where the Wild and the Blackhawks have cultivated quite the rivalry, thanks to three recent meetings in the Stanley Cup Playoffs.

Fans in Chicago are passionate about their Blackhawks, but they aren't threatening, which makes the road trip a fun one. While crowds in Philadelphia have earned a reputation as being a bit over-the-top—they once booed Santa Claus at a Philadelphia Eagles game—crowds in Chicago are generally more respectful of fans from out of town.

The experience at United Center is also unique. Not only is United Center the biggest arena in the league—it seats upwards of 21,000 people for a hockey game—the stadium itself is cavernous, which makes for one loud building when the Blackhawks are having a good night.

While the arena is not directly downtown, it's easily accessible via public transportation or ride-sharing services. Even on a weekend night, it's relatively inexpensive to get a ride from a downtown hotel to the arena. Where things can get spendy is getting into the building itself.

As of 2017, the Blackhawks had the fourth-most expensive average ticket cost in the NHL, trailing only the New York Rangers, Detroit Red Wings, and Toronto Maple Leafs, all fellow Original Six teams.

If you do get in, get there early. Jim Cornelison's rendition of "The Star-Spangled Banner" is absolutely legendary, as 21,000 fans clap and cheer while he sings, a tradition that dates back to the old Chicago Stadium. It's a must-see any time you make the trek to the United Center, no matter how many times you've been there.

If you're looking for a tasty meal before the game, you can't visit Chicago and not have some deep-dish pizza. Two spots with multiple locations downtown, Gino's East and Lou Malnati's, offer some of the best Chicago-style pizza in town and are very reasonable on the wallet.

While the trip is drivable, flights to Chicago out of Minneapolis–St. Paul are extremely affordable. Although flying in day of game is certainly possible, be sure to plan ahead and check the forecast. Winters in both the Twin Cities and in Chicago can be dicey, especially for air travel. They don't call it the Windy City for nothing. And while the origin of that moniker has nothing to do with the weather—at least that's what the locals will tell you—it's well earned.

Your best bet? Get to town a day early and partake in all that the city of Chicago has to offer.

16 Bertuzzi's Gaffe

During the Wild's magical 2003 run through the Stanley Cup Playoffs, a confluence of events helped pave the way for Minnesota to make an improbable run to the Western Conference Finals. Some came on the ice; others came off.

One of the most memorable, at least in the minds of players, was an off-the-cuff remark by Vancouver Canucks forward Todd Bertuzzi following a Game 4 win over the Wild in the second round.

Vancouver led the series 3–1 and was heading back home with a chance to close out the underdog Wild on home ice. After securing the win, the Canucks remained in St. Paul overnight and planned to fly back to Vancouver the following day. After a practice session at Xcel Energy Center, Canucks players walked out of the arena past a line of Wild fans waiting for a chance to purchase tickets for Game 6.

As legend has it, Bertuzzi looked at the fans and said, "Don't waste your time. There isn't going to be a Game 6."

Now the exact statement has never been verified; May of 2003 was long before the current social media or camera phone era, so his exact wording wasn't documented, but a number of fans heard the comment.

Through the grapevine, so did Wild players. "We caught wind of it," said former Wild forward Wes Walz. "Today on Twitter, that would be everywhere. I don't know how it got back to us, but it did. It'd be interesting to see how it got back to us. Not that we needed any more motivation, but that fueled us, it really did. I don't care what anybody says, nobody likes to be slighted like that.

Especially him, he had a big mouth, he wouldn't shut up on the ice.'"

Had the shoe been on the other foot, it's likely such a comment would have never been made, if only because Jacques Lemaire made a point of avoiding such controversy earlier in the same playoff run.

Following Richard Park's overtime goal against Colorado to win Game 6 in the first round, Lemaire didn't say much to players in the dressing room. One thing he was sure to tell his players was to keep their business close to the vest and not provide the heavily favored Avalanche with any sort of bulletin board material they could use the following night in Denver. "He talked to us for about a minute, 'No bulletin board, no nothing. Answer the questions the right way, it's all business,'" Walz said. "Then he walked out of the room. There was no high-fiving anybody."

Minnesota responded in a big way following the comment, smoking the Canucks 7-2 in Vancouver in Game 5, then scoring a 5–1 win back in front of its home crowd in Game 6, forcing a seventh game in British Columbia.

The Wild fell behind 2–0 at 12:30 of the second period but rallied with four unanswered goals—including three in the third period—to win the game 4–2, capping a second consecutive comeback from a 3–1 series deficit.

Minnesota remains the only team in NHL history to overcome a pair of such deficits in a single playoff run. "It gave us a lot of juice when Bertuzzi did that," Walz said. "That fueled us for sure."

17

Moose Goheen

Perhaps the best hockey player to ever come from the state of Minnesota is one who never played in the National Hockey League.

Born in St. Paul but raised in White Bear Lake six years before the turn of the 20th century, Francis Xavier Goheen played three seasons for the St. Paul Athletic Club before a two-year stint in Europe during World War I. After returning from the war, Goheen played 12 more seasons of hockey in his hometown, spurning offers to leave and play in the NHL.

Goheen did it all during his time on the ice, playing forward, defense, and rover in the seven-man game. He helped the St. Paul Athletic Club to a pair of MacNaughton Cups in 1916 and 1920. The trophy, which is now awarded to the regular season champion of the Western Collegiate Hockey Association, was—at the time—symbolic of American amateur hockey dominance.

After returning from the war, Goheen served his country again, this time skating for the Americans in the Olympic Games of 1920, helping the U.S. to a silver medal by scoring seven goals in four games. It was the first time hockey was played as a sport in the Olympics.

Goheen could have skated for the U.S. again four years later but choose to pass on the opportunity because he didn't want to leave behind his job at Northern States Power Company. It was to be a common refrain.

Drafted by the Boston Bruins, Goheen was offered a contract by the Toronto Maple Leafs. However, his job with NSP and his spot with the Athletic Club was enough to keep him at home.

The Athletic Club team turned professional in 1926 (becoming the minor league St. Paul Saints), and Goheen went with them, finally joining the pro ranks for the first time in his career. His two best seasons came in his later years with the Saints in 1925–26 when he scored 13 goals and 10 assists in 36 games and in 1927–28 when he tallied 19 goals and 5 assists in 39 games.

A star athlete who played three sports (football, baseball, and hockey) Goheen briefly attended Valparaiso University in Indiana. His slap shot goal in a 1924 game may be one of the earliest such achievements.

Goheen was elected to the Hockey Hall of Fame in Toronto in 1952, becoming just the second American (Hobey Baker was the first) and first Minnesotan to be inducted to that elite shrine. He was named to the Minnesota Sports Hall of Fame in 1958 and in 1973 was part of the inaugural class inducted into the United States Hockey Hall of Fame at Eveleth, Minnesota.

18 Flip of a Coin

The course upon which the Wild franchise would set was decided by the flip of a coin.

In the run up to the expansion draft and the NHL Entry Draft in 2000, the league was finishing its four-team expansion that moved the NHL from 26 to 30 teams between 1998 and 2000.

The Nashville Predators were the 27th club in 1998, followed by the Atlanta Thrashers the following year. Minnesota and the Columbus Blue Jackets were joining together in 2000, so their expansion draft would end up being much different than the first two. For one, they'd be competing for the same crop of players in the expansion portion of the proceedings. "You couldn't really predict who you were going to get because the other guys could take them," said former Wild general manager Doug Risebrough. "I look back on it, and the most critical thing was the entry draft."

The Wild and Blue Jackets were also drafting third and fourth overall in the entry draft, which was an important distinction; most NHL experts believed—and it's proven accurate with the benefit of hindsight—the 2000 Draft was a three-man draft at the top.

Who would get pick No. 3 and who would get pick No. 4 (the top pick in the expansion draft) was left to a coin flip by NHL deputy commissioner Bill Daly. "He was tossing the coin with all these cameras around," Risebrough said. "And Bill is as calm as a cucumber; he doesn't get anxious about anything. But for some reason, he was really nervous about this coin toss, and the sweat was dripping down."

The coin had a Wild logo on one side and a Blue Jackets emblem on the other. Daly flipped it high in the air, only to see it hit the table, bounce off, and land on the floor near Risebrough's feet.

The Wild GM looked down and saw his own logo up. "Then he [Daly] scoops it up and says, 'It has to land on the table,'" Risebrough said. "I wasn't about to make a big deal out of it because he's in charge. I just thought, *What are the chances of this coming up twice?*"

Daly flipped the coin again, keeping it on the table on the second try. Sure enough, it landed with the Wild logo showing.

Elated, Risebrough chose for Minnesota to select third in the entry draft and allow Columbus the top pick in the expansion draft.

The Wild, of course, picked Marian Gaborik with the third pick in the 2000 Draft. Columbus, which picked goaltender Rick Tabaracci first in the expansion draft, chose defenseman Rostislav Klesla one pick after Minnesota nabbed Gaborik.

Klesla ended up being a solid player in the NHL, finishing his career in 2013–14 after playing in 659 games in the league, including 515 with the Blue Jackets, scoring 41 goals and 133 points while posting a minus-50 in 13 seasons in the league.

Gaborik, selected after goaltender Rick DiPietro and forward Dany Heatley, played eight seasons with the Wild and left as the franchise leader in goals, assists, and points upon signing as a free agent with the New York Rangers in 2009. He's played in more than 1,000 NHL games with five teams.

19 Wes Walz

Wes Walz has often said that if not for the Minnesota Wild, he likely never would have played another NHL game following the 1995–96 season.

Walz was a junior hockey star, who once had a pair of 100-plus-points seasons for the Lethbridge Hurricanes in the Western Hockey League. His final season there, Walz scored 54 goals and had 140 points, a campaign which came a few months after he was drafted in the third round of the 1989 NHL Draft by the Boston Bruins.

The Calgary native debuted the following year in the NHL, playing in just two games but scoring a goal and assisting on another.

Walz played in 56 more games with Boston in 1990–91, tallying eight goals and eight assists.

But that was the high-water mark for Walz during his first stint in the world's best hockey league. "I was always kind of surprised that they drafted me," Walz said. "Playing in that small rink in Boston, it wasn't really built for a guy that could skate. I really had a difficult time that first year. I really should have played that whole first year in Portland [of the AHL]. My career went sideways pretty early."

In 1991–92, he played in 15 games with Boston before he was traded to Philadelphia. After his two-game run there, he spent an entire season in the American Hockey League before returning

Wild center Wes Walz controls the puck during a January 2002 game against the Montreal Canadiens, in which Walz had two goals and an assist.

home to play for the Flames in 1993–94. Two seasons and 92 games later, Walz was on the move again, playing just two contests with the Detroit Red Wings in 1995–96.

Suddenly, his career was at a crossroads. With his NHL opportunities limited, Walz went overseas to Switzerland, where he played four seasons in the National League, the top league in that country. "I'd been up and down so much in the minors, I just decided to go to Europe," Walz said. "It was supposed to be just for one year, just to get away from things. I was getting paid pretty well to be an import, and we had two young children. Then one year turned into four."

While there, the NHL expanded by four, first with the Nashville Predators in 1998 and the Atlanta Thrashers in 1999 before the Wild and Columbus Blue Jackets joined the ranks in time for the 2000–01 season. "I had quietly agreed to another four-year deal with Lugano," Walz said. "I was pretty much prepared to ride off into the sunset and play out the rest of my career in Switzerland."

The summer after Walz's fourth season in Switzerland, Doug Risebrough called him to see if he had any interest in returning to North America. Risebrough was the assistant general manager in Calgary when Walz was there, so they had a bit of a past. "I always thought his skill set in the NHL didn't align with the kind of person he was," Risebrough said. "When I had Wes [in Calgary], I always thought he was a fast player who could check. It was just the right fit at the right time in his career."

But with security and a good salary in Switzerland, Walz wanted one main concession: he wanted a one-way contract.

The Wild initially offered Walz a two-way contract anyway, and Walz told his agent to not even bother responding. "I was always on a two-way, and I would outplay guys on one-ways, and I would always be the one to go down," Walz said. "I said, 'I'm not fighting that fight anymore.' I was comfortable over there, I was 30 years old, I was making huge money over there to play in Switzerland. I didn't have that much pride in that I was going to come back for financial reasons.

"I didn't want to waste anybody's time. Then Doug stepped up to the plate and gave me a one-way. It wasn't big money; I was actually making less money playing for the Wild my first year. I would have made 60 percent more money playing in Europe, but I wanted the opportunity to come back and prove myself. Doug put his neck on the line for me."

Walz made a big impression on hard-nosed coach Jacques Lemaire in his first training camp. The one-time offensive juggernaut in junior hockey had transformed his game in his second go-round in the NHL, as Walz quickly became one of Lemaire's most trusted two-way forwards.

A few days into his first training camp, Walz was headed home from the team's temporary practice arena at Parade Ice Garden when Lemaire, standing outside smoking a cigarette, called the veteran forward over. "He said he was very impressed with how I was skating and how I was playing," Walz said. "He basically told me I'm going to make the team."

Then he asked his eager, speedy forward for a favor. "He asked me to slow down," Walz said. "I was skating too fast. I wanted to get noticed, and he knew I could skate. He just asked me to slow down and play a little bit smarter, especially in our own zone." Walz knew exactly what Lemaire was asking of him; he wanted Walz to serve as his checking center.

He played in all 82 games in his first season back in North America, something he had never done his first time in the NHL. His 18 goals were also a career high, though he scored seven of those shorthanded, a perfect illustration of his role with the expansion Wild.

Walz was a staple in the Wild's lineup for six seasons, playing in at least 80 games two more times, while also donning the C as captain on multiple occasions during the team's early tradition of the rotating captain. He chipped in 30 or more points in four of his six full seasons in Minnesota and became a fan favorite.

Still, it's his two-way work that ranks him among the most popular players in franchise history.

20 The 2000 NHL Draft

The Wild held the third overall selection in the 2000 NHL Draft, but there was only one player the club had atop its draft board on the floor of the Saddledome in Calgary, Alberta.

That player was Trencin, Slovakia, native Marian Gaborik.

Experts pegged the draft as a three-man race at the top, with goaltender Rick DiPietro and University of Wisconsin forward Dany Heatley joining Gaborik as the consensus top picks.

A few days earlier, the Wild won a coin flip with fellow expansion club Columbus for the right to pick third. Had it lost that coin toss, it's quite likely Minnesota would have been relegated to picking fourth overall. "We didn't know who we were going to get," said Wild general manager at-the-time Doug Risebrough. "We were picking third and we knew we were going to get one of the three. Gaborik was No. 1 on our list."

It's not entirely unheard of for a GM or coach to say after the fact, "Well, we got the top guy on our draft board picking third." No manager in their right mind would admit to taking their third favorite player in a three-man draft. But when you hear Risebrough mention Gaborik as the top player on his draft board, you tend to believe him.

A lot more than simply scouting the player and looking at his stats went into picking Gaborik with the first selection in franchise history. "For the team to have a chance and for the fans to believe in the team, it had to be a team that fans would instantly relate to," Risebrough said. "At least if we got skaters, people would feel, 'Yeah, this team is going in the right direction' because it was inherent in their hockey knowledge and their hockey blood." Risebrough thought about the proud lineage of skaters that had come from the state of Minnesota and figured that if the player himself couldn't come from the state, a player that could skate like the wind would at least remind locals of the kind of hockey they were used to watching.

As gifted as Heatley would be—up close for Wild fans later in his career—Gaborik was the unquestioned best skater in the draft. So when the New York Islanders went goaltender first overall, and the Atlanta Thrashers picked Heatley second, Risebrough and the Wild practically sprinted to the stage to pick Gaborik third. "It added a hope to what we would be one day," Risebrough said. "It added kind of an instant gratification for the people that would watch the game. And as it turned out, Marian wasn't the fastest guy on the team; it was Wes Walz. It became a fast team, which carried us."

But the Wild weren't done taking impact players in its first draft, as it picked defenseman Nick Schultz with the third pick in round two.

Schultz played one year of junior hockey but made his debut with the Wild as a 19-year-old in 2001. The plan wasn't for him to play in 52 games as a rookie, but more to get his feet wet in the league and practice on a daily basis with older, veteran players.

But Schultz was simply too good to keep in the press box. "I was lucky as an expansion GM; I didn't have a team, so I wasn't watching my team. I was out watching hockey games," Risebrough said. "I got a chance to see a lot of young players myself, and what I liked about Nick was his intelligence for the game, his competitiveness, and he just wanted to win, in a quiet way. He was an honest, hardworking player."

That mentality fit in perfectly with the first few teams Risebrough put on the ice, ones that earned the tags of honest and hardworking. "We just tried to make sure these guys were developing the right way," Risebrough said. "In Nick's case, we decided that he would stay, and we told him he wouldn't play all the games, but he would practice, and it would be good for his development. Typical Nick, he played more than we thought he would."

21 Watch a Game in Winnipeg

One road trip fans need to plan ahead for is Winnipeg, Manitoba, to watch the Jets and Wild square off at Bell MTS Place. For starters, because the game is in Canada, you need a passport (or a passport card if you're making the trip by car) to get across the border. Also, it's increasingly difficult to find a ticket to watch a game in the Jets' tiny home arena. With a capacity of just over 15,000 fans, Bell MTS Place is one of the NHL's smallest home buildings. But don't let its lack of seating fool you; make your way into this hornet's nest and you'll be taking in one of the loudest in-game experiences the league has to offer.

While weather can be tricky for this road trip, the average fan from the Twin Cities is encouraged to load up the car for a day trip. With clear roads and good weather, the car ride north from Minneapolis can be made in about seven hours. It's easy too, as the fastest route there brings you northwest on Interstate 94, straight north on Interstate 29 to the border, and to Provincial Highway

75 once in Canada. It's four lanes all the way, with speed limits ranging from 70 to 80 mph in the U.S., and 110 km/h (around 70 mph) in Manitoba.

Airfare to Winnipeg from Minneapolis can range in the hundreds of dollars or more per ticket, depending on when reservations are made. The airport in Winnipeg is a 10-minute drive from most of the hotels in and around the building.

If it's winter when you make the trip, bundle up. The city of Winnipeg is in the middle of the Canadian prairie, and it gets quite windy. Legend has it that the corner of Portage and Main—known as the crossroads of Canada—in the heart of downtown is the windiest spot in North America, and it's just a stone's throw from Bell MTS Place.

Once you're settled in town, there is a vast network of skyways and tunnels to keep you warm and out of the wind should you choose to use them. Hearty fans will have many Tim Horton's locations to choose from to refuel with a coffee or some Timbits, a Canadian tradition.

Winnipeg is also home to some of the best poutine in Canada. The Shark Club Gaming Centre, attached via skyway to the arena, is a great place to watch other games if you're in town on an off night. A tall beer isn't cheap, but remember, the prices are higher in Canada because of the exchange rate.

Looking for an underrated lunch spot? Bailey's Restaurant and Lounge is within walking distance from the arena and stands just steps from Portage and Main. The soup and salad is fantastic and will cost you less than $20 Canadian.

Moxie's, connected to Bell MTS Place, and Earl's, are Canadian staples with solid atmosphere and good food as well.

On game day, bring your earplugs. While the building itself is small, there isn't a bad seat in the house. A fan could sit in the very last row of the arena and still have a great view of the action. Bell MTS Place has been recently remodeled, and there are no longer

any obstructed view seats, so buy your tickets without worry...
if you can find them. Winnipeg's attendance numbers, at least in
terms of percentage of seats filled, is among the best in the league
each and every season.

If you can get in, the fan experience is outstanding. Few cities
in the world are more passionate about their team than Winnipeg is
of the Jets. The Canadian hospitality is second to none, and while
they won't cheer for your favorite team, they'll certainly welcome
you to enjoy the game.

St. Paul Civic Center

On the exact site of the Xcel Energy Center stood the first home
of professional hockey in downtown St. Paul: the iconic St. Paul
Civic Center.

After opening on January 1, 1973, the Civic Center served as
the epicenter of Minnesota hockey for more than 25 years. Home
of the Minnesota Fighting Saints of the World Hockey Association,
then the Minnesota Moose of the IHL, the old barn most promi-
nently served as home of the Minnesota State High School League
boys' hockey state tournament. Numerous other events, including
the WCHA Final Five and the NCAA Frozen Four, also took place
the arena, but it was the high school state tournament that was
most associated with the building.

Despite being a hockey arena, it was not designed with the best
hockey sight lines in mind. Its famously round shape proved to be
an obstacle when sitting close to the ice; an oval ice sheet in the
middle of a circular arena made it difficult for fans in some of the
very best seats to see large parts of the scoring zones.

The solution? Clear boards. The most unique feature of the Civic Center was its clear dasher boards, which allowed fans to see from the top of the glass all the way down to the ice surface itself.

For two decades, the clear boards became the trademark of the building until the IHL's Minnesota Moose installed white dashers in order to sell advertising, a decision that highlighted the arena's poor sight lines. The Moose weren't long for the Twin Cities, however, staying in St. Paul just two years before heading north to Winnipeg.

St. Paul Civic Center had a seating capacity of 16,000 for hockey enough for an NHL team to locate there. City and state leaders tried to lure the Jets to the arena in the mid-1990s before they eventually moved to Phoenix. After the North Stars left in 1993, expansion whispers also swirled around the building.

Ultimately, the arena's shortcomings helped spur the push for a new arena at the corner of Kellogg Boulevard and West Seventh Street. That new arena would eventually be Xcel Energy Center.

After Minnesota was awarded an NHL expansion franchise in 1997, the St. Paul Civic Center was torn down to make room for Xcel Energy Center. The new building has allowed St. Paul to remain the center of the hockey world in Minnesota.

23 Bruce Boudreau

Bruce Boudreau's hiring with the Wild in May of 2016 came about rather unexpectedly.

After dismissing coach Mike Yeo the previous February, Minnesota had promoted the coach of its American Hockey League affiliate in Iowa, John Torchetti, to fill out the remainder of the 2015–16 season. Minnesota rallied to make the playoffs before losing in six games to the Dallas Stars in the first round, ending its season.

Halfway across the country, Boudreau was leading the Anaheim Ducks against the underdog Nashville Predators in a playoff series. The Ducks, perpetually one of the NHL's best teams under Boudreau, couldn't finish off their opponents from the Music City, eventually losing at home in Game 7, marking its fourth disappointing exit from the postseason of the Boudreau era.

A few days later, despite posting a regular season record of 208–104–40, the Ducks decided to let Boudreau go.

Still in the midst of its coaching search (along with the Calgary Flames and Ottawa Senators) the Wild maneuvered for an interview. But for one reason or another, Minnesota seemed like a long shot.

One of Boudreau's sons lives in the Rocky Mountains outside Calgary and regularly visited his dad when his teams came to town to play. His daughter, pregnant at the time, resides in Ottawa, and the Canadian capital is just a short drive from Boudreau's hometown of St. Catharine's, Ontario.

Boudreau's only history in Minnesota was a short-lived (and less than memorable) stop in St. Paul in 1975, when he played 30 games with the Minnesota Fighting Saints in the World Hockey Association.

His life in Minnesota wasn't easy. A young kid on an older team, Boudreau was hazed incessantly. "It was a bad experience," Boudreau wrote in his book, *Gabby: Confessions of a Hockey Lifer.* "In those days, it was common practice for the older guys to single out first-round draft picks and treat them rough. You went from being top dog to being a piece of garbage. I wasn't used to it and I didn't like it."

Boudreau wrote about one specific incident that put him in the hospital. "They pinned me down on a gurney and tied my legs and arms," Boudreau wrote. "They shaved my head and pubic area. Then they put turpentine on the cuts and smeared black tar on my groin and chest. They finished by gluing my armpits and left me lying there bawling like a baby until the trainer came and took me to the hospital."

It was a trying time for Boudreau, an uber-talented prospect from the Toronto area who, if not for a rogue streaking incident, may have been a high first-round pick in the NHL as well. "If I didn't love the game so much, I would have quit after that day," Boudreau wrote. "It's one of the reasons I've never liked initiations. I've never cut another guy's hair."

Luckily for Boudreau, his first stop in Minnesota was short-lived. He played just 30 games for the Fighting Saints before the team went under and he moved on. For two decades, Boudreau lived a nomadic lifestyle as a player, suiting up for 13 different teams in three separate countries.

His coaching career began much the same way his playing career ended, moving from town to town. His first head-coaching gig in the American Hockey League was in Lowell, Massachusetts; followed by Manchester, New Hampshire; and finally, Hershey, Pennsylvania, until a midseason promotion to the Washington Capitals in 2007 gave him his start in the NHL coaching ranks.

Four-plus years in Washington and a similar stint in Anaheim paved his way back to Minnesota and the job with the Wild in what has to be one of the most fascinating journeys in the sport today.

It's a road that has certainly helped make Boudreau one of the game's true characters—and despite a rough start continuing an odyssey that began in Minnesota more than four decades ago, Boudreau has said he hopes this is where his journey in the sport one day ends. "I told my wife this is the last place we're going," Boudreau said at his introductory press conference with the Wild. "I'm going to stay here and I hope it's a long time."

24 Eveleth

Three hours north of the Twin Cities of Minneapolis and St. Paul sits a cauldron of hockey history. Home of the United States Hockey Hall of Fame, tiny Eveleth, Minnesota—population 3,600—has one of the richest hockey pasts of any town in the United States.

There was a time when Eveleth, the gateway to Minnesota's famed Iron Range, was more than twice as large as it is today. Founded around the turn of the century and named after Erwin Eveleth, a timber magnate, the town was booming during the 1920s and 1930s after iron ore was discovered in the area.

Once iron ore was discovered nearby in 1895, it didn't take long for immigrants from all over Europe to settle the area. Eveleth became a blue-collar mining town, and hockey quickly became its favorite pastime.

The first official record of hockey being played in the area is from January 23, 1903. At Fayal Pond, on what locals referred to as O'Hare's Skating Rink, Eveleth went head-to-head against Two Harbors, a game the visitors won 5–2.

Popularity of the sport grew exponentially after that, and by the Great Depression, Eveleth had perhaps the most powerful team in the state.

But hockey was also big business in town.

In the 1920s Eveleth mayor Victor Essling was the driving force behind a brand-new, state-of-the-art arena. On January 1, 1922, the Hippodrome opened for business. It's 3,000-seat capacity could fit nearly half the town inside its walls. "The Hipp," as it's still called today, was nicknamed the "Madison Square Garden of the Northland."

In its first game, the Eveleth Reds of the United States Amateur Hockey Association packed the arena to capacity and defeated the Duluth Hornets by a 10–6 score.

With the National Hockey League still a few years away from its founding, the USAHA was the highest level of hockey in America at the time, and Eveleth's Reds played—and won—against teams from cities more than 10 times its size, including Pittsburgh and Cleveland. During its first year of existence in 1920–21, the Reds won the MacNaughton Cup as league champions.

Unfortunately for the team, and the league, the USAHA didn't last. By the end of the 1920s, the league—and the Reds—no longer existed. But the success of the Reds helped captivate the town even more, laying the foundation for the high school's success a decade later.

Once the NHL arrived in the mid-1920s, players from Eveleth played a big part in the early years of that league as well. During the 1930s, with just eight teams playing in the NHL, four of the goaltenders hailed from the town, earning Eveleth the nickname of "Goalie Town U.S.A."

Perhaps the best of the bunch, Frank Brimsek, aka "Mr. Zero," won the Calder Memorial Trophy as the NHL's Rookie of the Year in 1939 after helping the Boston Bruins to the Stanley Cup championship. He also won the Vezina Trophy that season and again in 1942 as the league's best goaltender.

One of the most successful teams to ever come from Eveleth was the junior college team in 1928–29. The team defeated schools from all around the country, including the University of Minnesota, Yale, and Harvard. The team was so successful that it was offered the opportunity to represent the United States at the 1928 Olympics. If not for a lack of funding, the school's team would have been America's team in Amsterdam.

The coach of that team, Cliff Thompson, also coached Eveleth High School, which won the first-ever Minnesota State High School League tournament in 1945. Prior to that, for more than a decade, the team was unstoppable, at one point during the late 1920s putting together a winning streak that lasted more than three years.

After World War II and once the state tournament was formed, Eveleth's powerhouse status was on display to a statewide audience. The Golden Bears won five of the first seven state championships and won 69 consecutive games over a four-year span.

Thompson finished his coaching career with a remarkable 534–26–9 record and helped guide the careers of several Hall of Famers, including Brimsek, John Mariucci, John Mayasich, and Willard Ikola, among a host of others.

It was largely because of Thompson that the tiny town of Eveleth has more members in the U.S. Hockey Hall of Fame than any other city in the nation, a big reason why the hall itself is located in such a remote locale.

25 The Rotating Captaincy

Captains in hockey, perhaps more than any other sport, are revered and reviled by a fan base.

Pittsburgh's Sidney Crosby and Chicago's Jonathan Toews have cultivated reputations as two of the very best leaders in the game, captains that guys follow through thick and thin.

In Minnesota, for more than a decade, that man has been Mikko Koivu. But despite being selected by the team in the first round of the 2001 NHL Draft and not debuting in the league until 2005, Koivu is actually the first permanent captain in franchise history.

Prior to 2008–09, when Koivu took over as the captain on a permanent basis, former Wild coach Jacques Lemaire used a rotating captaincy, meant as a reward for his players on a month-by-month basis. When the Wild hit the ice in 2000, it didn't have an obvious choice for captain. So Lemaire used the rotating captain as a way to motivate and reward guys who showed leadership or played the game the right way.

For some it was an honor they likely would have never achieved otherwise. "To wear the 'C' at the highest level of professional hockey, it's almost beyond words," former Wild forward Wes Walz told Ross Bernstein in the book *Wearing the C: Leadership Secrets from Hockey's Greatest Captains*. "To know that you have the confidence of the coaching staff and of the entire organization, it's a pretty incredible feeling. As a player, it's the ultimate feather in your cap. They believe in you as a player, as a guy for others to look up to and they admire your work ethic and preparation. It's very humbling."

Walz came to the Wild after playing four years in Switzerland. He was never the team's leading scorer or its biggest name, but because he played a tenacious style and thrived as Lemaire's checking center, he was able to earn the captain on multiple occasions during his time with the club. Even if he wasn't the captain on a given month, Walz was often wearing an A as an alternate captain.

No matter what letter you had on his chest, or if you didn't have one at all, having an extra bit of incentive every month to put your best foot forward never hurt. It also fueled some healthy competition between guys on the team. "I just tried to work as hard as I could and bust my ass every day. I didn't say a whole lot. Instead I just tried to let my actions do the talking for me. That was it," Walz told Bernstein. "If you did the right things and played the right way, this was [Lemaire's] way of thanking you as well as incentivizing you."

26 College Hockey Hotbed

Minnesota's moniker as the "State of Hockey" is a brilliant marketing slogan first unveiled shortly after NHL hockey returned to the state with the Wild. But it also has the benefit of being true.

Minnesota produces more NHL players than any other state in the United States with more than 50 skating in at least one league game during the 2017–18 regular season. And more are coming: 17 were selected in the 2017 NHL Draft in Chicago, meaning the future is bright.

Part of the influx of talent into the pro ranks comes from Minnesota's talent-rich feeder system, which starts at the youth levels and goes through high school and on to the college and junior hockey ranks.

For the past two decades, five Division I teams have called the state home—still short of both Michigan and Massachusetts, but all five Minnesota-based schools have proven they can win at the highest levels of college hockey. The University of Minnesota has won five national championships and is one of college hockey's flagship programs, with a history dating back nearly a century. The University of Minnesota-Duluth has won the national championship three times during the past decade and has become one of the college game's most consistent teams. St. Cloud State University was transformed from an afterthought into one of college's hockey's winningest programs by alum Bob Motzko, who led the Huskies to their first Frozen Four at the Division I level and won several conference championships before leaving for the Golden Gophers in 2018. Minnesota State University has been one of the most successful programs in the country during the regular season since 2012 when it hired Mike Hastings as its head coach. Longtime St. Louis Blues captain and current Boston Bruin David Backes is a MSU alum. Bemidji State University went to a Frozen Four in 2009 and has produced solid NHLers like Matt Read and Brad Hunt during its modern era.

As the NHL continues to cultivate talent from the college hockey ranks, Minnesota's NCAA teams will likely play an even bigger role in the future. New arenas in Duluth and Bemidji have reinvigorated the passion for hockey in those communities. Millions more have been spent to renovate arenas in St. Cloud and Mankato. For many, Minnesota's Mariucci Arena remains the center of the college hockey universe.

27 The Boogeyman

Few characters in the history of the Wild franchise have captured the imagination of fans quite like Derek Boogaard.

The 202nd overall pick in the 2001 NHL Draft, Boogaard was an imposing figure. He stood 6'7" and weighed 265 pounds. He played during an era when enforcers still had an important role, both on the ice and in the locker room.

In both settings, Boogaard was a beloved figure.

Boogaard played with three different teams in four years in the Western Hockey League, including the Regina Pats, the Prince George Cougars, and the Medicine Hat Tigers. He played in 174 games during that span and scored just three goals and 21 points. But he also racked up 670 penalty minutes and a reputation as one of the league's toughest players. "Derek was one of my most fond experiences in hockey," said former Wild general manager Doug Risebrough, the man who drafted Boogaard. "I saw Derek play and I thought, *He's got a chance*. He could skate, he was big, and he could be physical. It wasn't just about the fighting."

Boogaard had perhaps his best season of his junior career the year before he was drafted, posting a goal, eight assists, and a career-high 245 penalty minutes in 61 games, a total he wouldn't equal in any of his NHL seasons.

The Wild knew what it was getting in Boogaard but believed there was also something else there. The club knew it wasn't getting a guy who would ever likely produce many points offensively, but former Wild coach Jacques Lemaire believed it was also getting someone who could do more than simply drop the gloves.

"He just needed a chance," Risebrough said. Risebrough offered Boogaard a contract to turn pro prior to the 2002–03

Minnesota Wild left wing Derek Boogaard screens Edmonton Oilers goalie Jussi Markkanen, enabling right wing Mark Parrish's goal during the first period of an April 2007 game.

season, but on the advice of his agent, Boogaard turned the offer down and returned to his junior team in Medicine Hat.

Boogaard played in just 27 games that season and, almost immediately, regretted not turning pro. Risebrough recalled running into Boogaard at a Wild game in Calgary, where the towering player informed the GM he was no longer on the team in Medicine Hat. He wanted a chance to turn professional. "I said, 'I'll tell you what; I'll give you a chance, but you're starting at the lowest level possible and you're going to have to work your way up,'" Risebrough recalled. "He did that. He worked and worked and worked and he became a player and a very likable player."

Boogaard finished the season with the Louisiana Ice Gators in the ECHL, compiling 240 penalty minutes in just 33 games. He spent the next two seasons with the club's AHL affiliate in Houston.

Finally, more than four years after being drafted, Boogaard made his debut in the NHL, playing in 65 games in 2005–06. His rookie season was the only one in which he scored more than one goal in a single season, and they would be the only two goals he would score in five seasons with Minnesota.

Despite the dearth of offense, Boogaard had a cult-like following among fans, who would chant "BOOOOOGEY" any time he would set foot on the ice.

Perhaps his most memorable fight in the NHL came at Xcel Energy Center in October of 2006. Anaheim Ducks tough guy Todd Fedoruk chased Boogaard nearly 200 feet from Anaheim's defensive zone into the other end of the rink, goading Boogaard to drop the gloves. Unfortunately for Fedoruk, Boogaard eventually complied.

For a couple of seconds, the two traded quick blows until Boogaard, who had gotten Fedoruk to open his body with a couple of quick left-handed jabs, caved Fedoruk's face in with a quick right-handed cross.

The gasp inside the arena was audible. Fans gave Boogaard a loud standing ovation as he skated to the penalty box, his left hand in the air acknowledging the crowd.

Fedoruk went right to the bench, down the tunnel, and to the dressing room where he was treated for a shattered cheekbone. "Oh, my God, I feel so bad for him. I crushed his face. My hand is killing me," Boogaard said after the game, according to one account published for ESPN.com. "You never, ever wish that on somebody. But you've got to look at it in a different way, too. What happens if he had you in that position? Do you think he would let up? You know he wouldn't."

Fedoruk's injury was severe, and he knew it. "I didn't see it coming at all. I was in a bad position, and he hit me hard, hardest I've ever been hit. I instantly knew it was broken. I didn't lose consciousness, but I went straight on the ice. And I felt where it was, and my hand didn't rub my face normally. It was a little chunky and sharp in spots and there was a hole there about the size of a fist. Their bench was cheering like you do when your teammate gets a guy," Fedoruk would later tell the *New York Times*. "I remember skating by their bench. Their faces kind of lost expression because...you could see it. You could see the damage that was done because the cheekbone, it wasn't there anymore."

A year later, the Wild claimed Fedoruk on waivers. The two became close friends and even roommates on the road.

Boogaard played in 255 games with the Wild through the 2009–10 season before signing as a free agent with the New York Rangers. He skated in 22 games on Broadway, snapping a nearly five-year goal-scoring drought.

But years of life as an enforcer caught up with Boogaard, and the pain of countless injuries ended up cutting his life short when he died May 13, 2011, just 28 years of age. The cause of his death was ruled an accidental drug and alcohol overdose. Boogaard was recovering from a concussion at the time. "The fans liked Derek, the players liked Derek. He was a guy who was living his NHL dream," Risebrough said. "I give him all the credit; he was a guy who deserved a chance, got it, and he made the best of it."

28 Filling an Empty Cupboard

Optimism in Minnesota's hockey community was at an all-time high when the NHL announced in June of 1997 that the league was returning to Minnesota in the fall of 2000, a little more than seven years after the North Stars left town for Dallas.

The expansion team that would eventually become the Wild would have a brand-new, state-of-the-art arena in downtown St. Paul that would be widely viewed as one of the best in the league. But before the club would hire a general manager or a coach or field a team on the ice, there was the business of passing nearly three years' worth of time. And unlike the three other expansion markets that entered the league between 1998 and 2000, Minnesota didn't need to be introduced to the game of hockey itself.

In Nashville, Atlanta, and Columbus, hockey was a fringe sport. In Minnesota the game was a way of life, and emotions were still raw regarding the departure of the North Stars.

Good thing some of the team's first employees had plenty of time to make a new first impression. "I remember coming into… my office, and literally there was a pad of paper and a pencil and that was it," said Bill Robertson, the Wild's first vice president of communications. "There was nothing; no records, no files. That can be a challenge, and that can be an opportunity, and I looked at it like an opportunity to be like an artist, where you can paint the picture of how you want to do it…There was not a road map for those companies and how they wanted to do—certainly communications, community relations, broadcast—at that point. That was my job: to get those up and running and to do it in an efficient manner so 20 years later they can look at the archives and see exactly what happened."

Robertson had a great relationship with many of the local media in town from his years helping get the NBA's Minnesota Timberwolves off the ground. He also had a lot of time on his hands and carte blanche to do whatever he wanted to keep eyes focused on the new team. "The construction guys would be putting in a new beam at the arena, and Billy would have a press conference for it," said Jamie Spencer, the Wild's executive vice president of business development.

Rarely did Robertson miss an opportunity to get people talking about the new NHL team. When the plumbing was finished inside the brand-new Xcel Energy Center, Robertson invited local youth hockey teams to the arena to flush all the toilets and urinals at the same time, something Robertson called a "super flush." He made a big production out of it by inviting plenty of local media. "That one made Howard Stern's show," Spencer said with a laugh.

When the team announced that the club, then known as "Minnesota NHL" would finally have a nickname, the team did it in style, gathering thousands of fans at Aldrich Arena in suburban St. Paul, unveiling the name and secondary logo with a production that would make the WWE jealous.

Weeks later, when the Wild revealed its primary logo and home sweater, Robertson sent jerseys to major media outlets around the country. He couldn't have known the kind of traction it would get, but CNN did a segment on it, as did ESPN, in addition to all the local channels.

So while the three-year span between the announcement and first puck drop may have seemed long to some, it was a critical time in team history in helping to develop its own unique brand. "Some days I felt like P.T. Barnum because they were looking for me to create stunts," Robertson said. "We just tried to connect St. Paul to everything we were doing."

Robertson was also a key player in the first marketing of the Mighty Ducks of Anaheim before they began play in 1993. With the puck scheduled to drop in October of that year, Robertson said he was hired around Memorial Day, allowing him a summer to get things moving.

In Minnesota, he was brought in two and a half years before the first game. "When you have time to actually sit and drum up ideas, that's a good thing," Robertson said. "When you don't have time and you're just running from event to event and game to game… it's hard to do that. You need some creative time. I remember in the summer a few weeks before our first game, and [former team owner] Bob Naegele came into my office. He looked at me and said, 'Hey Billy, wouldn't it be great if we never had to play a game could just keep doing this?' It was the greatest line ever.

"Everything we did turned out really, really well. There weren't a lot of mistakes made, and we hired really exceptional people, and I give Bob and Jac [Sperling] a lot of credit for seeing and hiring the right people."

29 Jake Allen Dashes Minnesota's Hopes of a Long Playoff Run

Northwest Division championship aside, the Wild's best regular season came in coach Bruce Boudreau's first season behind the bench in 2016–17.

When Minnesota won its only division championship in franchise history in 2007–08, it did so by capturing only 44 wins in 82 games and finishing with 98 points in the standings. The year prior, Minnesota won four more games and had six more points, but finished second in the division behind Vancouver.

Hopes were high when Boudreau took over. The veteran coach had won four consecutive Pacific Division titles with the Anaheim

Ducks between 2013 and 2016. Prior to that, he had won four consecutive Southeast Division titles with the Washington Capitals between 2008 and 2011.

Even the 2011–12 season, which he split between Washington and Anaheim, Boudreau posted a record of 39–32–9. When he was hired to coach the Wild in May of 2016, the expectation was that Boudreau would have the veteran team ready to roll.

The addition of veteran centerman Eric Staal gave the Wild a deep roster of forwards and an experienced core on defense. Goaltender Devan Dubnyk was one of the best in the league since being acquired in a trade with the Coyotes a year and a half prior.

But Minnesota didn't have the start to the season it wanted. The Wild won just 11 of its first 23 games, and as the calendar turned to December, the team was under .500.

An overtime win in Edmonton on December 4 turned its entire season around. Minnesota wouldn't lose again until New Year's Eve, rattling off a franchise record 12-game winning streak in between. In an 19-game stretch between December 4 and January 15, the Wild won 17 of a possible 19 games. It opened up a double-digit point lead on the Chicago Blackhawks for the top spot in the Central Division.

A second division championship seemed all but assured as the month of March began. Minnesota won each of its first two games out of its bye week, ending February on a positive note. But a 1–0 loss to Columbus on March 2 was a sign of things to come. The Wild would lose 11 of its next 14 after that.

Minnesota closed its regular season with wins in five of its final six games, but any hopes of a division title were dashed by the March swoon. The Wild finished second in the Central Division and in the first round played the third-place St. Louis Blues led by former Wild coach Mike Yeo, who had been fired by the team just over a year earlier.

Despite earning home ice in the first round for just the second time in franchise history—and the third overall—the Wild couldn't overcome a red-hot goaltender. St. Louis' Jake Allen stymied the Wild at every turn, especially early in the series in a pair of 2–1 wins for the visitors.

Allen stopped 51 shots in Game 1, then 23 more in Game 2 as St. Louis brought a 2–0 lead back to its home rink.

In Game 3 the Wild outshot the Blues for the third consecutive game, but Allen was up to the task again, making 40 saves in a 3–1 win. Minnesota earned its only win in Game 4, sending the series back to Minnesota for a Game 5.

Allen again stole the show, making 34 saves as the Blues clinched the series with an overtime goal by Magnus Paajarvi.

Like that, the Wild's 49-win, 106-point regular season (each franchise records) was done. "[I] told them I was proud of their effort for the year," Boudreau said, following the loss in Game 5. "I know this is the part of the year that everybody including myself hates the most, when you put eight months into something and you don't get what you want. They never quit all year. When things were going bad, they still never quit, they kept pushing."

Despite a massive edge in the shot chart and in possession time in the series, Allen was the difference in eliminating Minnesota. "We outshot them," Wild captain Mikko Koivu succinctly put it after the series had ended. "I don't know scoring chances, I'm not a big stat guy, but I thought we had the momentum there for the most part, and it seemed like they had that one chance and they put it in."

"Usually you remember what you last saw, so, unfortunately, we're going to remember getting knocked out in five games," added Wild forward Zach Parise.

30 Roli the Goalie

Of all the things Dwayne Roloson has done in his NHL career, the first thing that comes to mind for Wild PR maven Aaron Sickman was something he did off the ice during his four-year stint in Minnesota.

Roloson did an intermission interview during a nationally televised game—not of a game he was the backup—but of one he was playing in. Although it's commonplace to see a goal scorer or a team captain join a broadcast for a quick hit before retreating to the dressing room, it's virtually unheard of for a goaltender to do so.

But when Sickman approached the charismatic goaltender, Roloson—perhaps surprisingly—said it wasn't a problem. "I'm not sure Jacques Lemaire would have obliged had I asked him," Sickman said.

But that's just the kind of guy Roloson was: carefree, fun-loving, and easygoing, a dressing room favorite of many of his teammates through the years.

Like so many players from the era that were perhaps on their last legs as NHLers, Roloson was another who may have never played another game in the league if not for the expansion of 1998–2000.

After a four-year college career at the University of Massachusetts-Lowell, Roloson began his time in the NHL with the Calgary Flames, playing in 31 games as a rookie in 1996–97. It was Doug Risebrough, who would later sign him in Minnesota, who inked him to his first contract with the Flames.

He played in 39 more with the Flames the following season before moving on to the Buffalo Sabres, where he played in 18 games in 1998–99 and 14 more the following season.

It was a trend that didn't seem to be working in his favor. Roloson was selected by the Columbus Blue Jackets in the Expansion Draft in 2000, but rather than sign with the Wild's expansion cousin, Roloson signed a deal to play for the St. Louis Blues.

Thought to be headed to the Blues as a backup, Roloson said he had a strong training camp. It didn't matter, as St. Louis assigned him to its AHL team in Worcester, Massachusetts, where he would stay for the whole season.

At that point, Roloson wasn't sure he'd ever make it to the NHL again. "When I went back to the minors in Worcester, I was thinking I was done," Roloson said. "We were going to give that one year—my wife and I had just gotten married. She was pregnant with our firstborn. At the time, it was sort of a play out this year and we'll reevaluate and figure out where we want to go with our lives."

Both Roloson and his wife, Melissa, held college degrees. Melissa's in chemical engineering, so the family didn't have to rely on hockey in future years. And with his playing time dwindling and his statistics going in the wrong direction, the family was prepared to move on.

But after watching his goals-against average hover in the high twos and his save percentage dip below 90 percent in Buffalo, Roloson got a chance to play every night, an opportunity that he said turned his career around.

Roloson's season in Worcester was outstanding, to the tune of a 2.17 goals against and a .929 save percentage in 52 games played.

That season gave him a new opportunity in the NHL, specifically with the Wild, one which he would use to add another decade to his professional playing career. "It was a blessing in disguise," Roloson said of his time in the minors. "I played pretty much every game, had lots of success. It gave me a chance to reestablish myself."

In 143 games with Minnesota over the next three seasons, Roloson posted a .921 save percentage and a sparkling 2.16 goals against, including a 1.88 goals against and .933 save percentage mark in 2003–04.

Twice with Minnesota he finished among the top nine in voting for the Vezina Trophy awarded to the best goaltender in the league. "Once I got there, I realized just how smart of a hockey guy Jacques was," Roloson said. "I learned so much in my time in Minnesota, how I thought about the game and thinking outside the box."

The NHL lockout that wiped out the 2005–06 season ended Roloson's chance to build on his best season, and when hockey returned in the fall of 2005, Roloson had just 24 games remaining in his Wild career.

That year, at the trade deadline, he was dealt to the Edmonton Oilers in exchange for a first-round draft pick. Roloson would go on to help the Oilers to the Stanley Cup Final that year and he played three more seasons in Edmonton.

Roloson retired from the NHL in 2012 at the age of 42, having played in 606 career games, but his .919 save percentage and 2.28 goals-against average in 167 games with the Wild were his best years in the league.

31 X Marks the Spot

For nearly 20 years, Xcel Energy Center has served as a blueprint for any number of facilities and arenas in North America. When it opened in 2000, the arena was unlike almost any arena built before it.

The 1990s saw an arena boom in the National Hockey League. Between 1993 and 1999, 18 of the NHL's current arenas opened. For comparison, when Detroit's Little Caesars Arena opened in the fall of 2017, it was just the ninth new building to open in the 17 seasons since Xcel's debut.

Although each of those buildings finished and opened in the 1990s has a different look and feel on the outside, most share many of the same traits and characteristics on the inside: concession areas and concourses that are closed off from the arena and playing surface itself. It makes the building feel as though it has two separate areas: the fans in the concourse and the fans in their seats.

Xcel Energy Center was one of the first of its kind to incorporate an open-style concourse. If you're standing in line waiting for food or a drink, you can hear and see what is happening inside the arena bowl. You don't have to walk through a tunnel to get to your seat.

It's part of the reason why Xcel Energy Center is still considered one of the best in the world. Many out-of-town visitors covering a game marvel at the fact that the building still looks and feels like it's new. It looks and feels that way because in many respects it is.

While Xcel Energy Center was the first of its kind in the NHL, it was actually inspired by a different sports venue about five years older: Denver's Coors Field. Like Xcel, Coors Field was designed by HOK Sports Facilities Group in Kansas City, Missouri. When

St. Paul approached the company for an arena for the Wild, Ray Chandler, the HOK principal in charge of the ballpark in Denver, was a key player. "He took us out to see Coors Field, which he had designed," said Bob Naegele, the Wild's original team owner. "Our challenge to him was, 'Ray, can you compose us an indoor venue that matches what we just experienced at Coors Field?' That became the target. And he did it."

Arena construction has slowed in recent years around the NHL, and because Xcel was on the forefront of modern arena design, it feels much newer than it actually is. It helps that some of the new buildings erected since Xcel opened—Gila River Arena in Glendale, Arizona; Prudential Center in Newark, New Jersey; and PPG Paints Arena in Pittsburgh, Pennsylvania—were all designed in large part to mimic what the Wild were able to accomplish in building Xcel Energy Center. "Others have tried to imitate it, but it doesn't have the heart of the State of Hockey," Naegele said. "They are just buildings [in other towns], but ours does have that soul. It's gotta be the cleanest arena in the league because there is a pride and an ownership by every employee. It's evident."

Other newer facilities—like T-Mobile Arena in Las Vegas, Detroit's Little Caesars, and Rogers Place in Edmonton, Alberta— have their own unique look but have incorporated the open concept concourse spearheaded in St. Paul.

When Xcel Energy Center was being built, it was a big risk to put such an asset in St. Paul. The city had fallen on hard times, and the area around the arena looked nothing like the vibrant, bustling neighborhood it does now. West Seventh Street, now filled with bars and restaurants, was like a ghost town.

Once the arena went up and the Wild came to town, the whole mood in the city changed. "We're so excited about the rejuvenation of St. Paul," Naegele said. "What the arena has done for, not only the status of the city, but for the state of Minnesota is great. The venue just embraces everything."

32 All Hands on Deck

With the advent of the legal negotiating window, teams are now able to secure the parameters of a contract with a free agent a couple of days before July 1.

Perhaps that would have saved the holiday for more than a few Wild employees in 2012. Back then teams were not allowed to contact free agents until July 1, which meant free agents like Ryan Suter and Zach Parise were going to have plenty of suitors lined up at the start of business.

Wild general manager Chuck Fletcher, team president Matt Majka, and owner Craig Leipold knew Minnesota was going to be aggressive in pursuing both players but had tried not to entertain too many thoughts of being able to secure both.

From a business standpoint, the Wild had made projections on how many season tickets it could sell if it landed Suter and how many it could sell if it signed Parise. Few had taken much time to calculate the potential windfall that would take place had it signed both.

As news began to get out that the Wild had pulled off one of the biggest coups in the history of NHL free agency, it became all hands on deck in the ticketing office. Majka had asked a few staffers, including Maria Troje, to stick around for a few hours just in case. "I didn't know anything, but I told her, 'Can you just be available, in case something happens?'" Majka recalled.

Once the Parise and Suter contracts came across the fax machine signed, Majka ran upstairs at the Wild's offices and let Troje and her sales crew know. She quickly got on the phone, looking for anyone available to come in. "People were coming in off the lake, in off the golf course," Majka said. "Other employees started hearing about it when it got announced and people just started flocking in because they wanted to be here."

As news broke on social media, phones began ringing off the hook. Anyone able to pick them up was asked to step in. That meant even Majka was answering phones and taking orders. "I was happy to that day because we needed it," Majka said.

The phones that began ringing that day kept on ringing for the rest of the summer. Minnesota's dwindling season-ticket base, which had been dipping for several seasons, suddenly surged. Its waiting list for tickets was reestablished. "It was a crazy summer," Majka said. "And we needed it. We were in a tough spot. But we were a better hockey team on the ice and a more unified organization. We were transformed."

33 Zach Parise

When Zach Parise joined Ryan Suter as members of the Minnesota Wild on July 4, 2012, Parise immediately gave the franchise something it had never had in its previous decade-plus of existence.

During an entire management cycle, the Wild shied away from dogged pursuit of Minnesotans to fill out its roster. Of course, a few local boys played under general manager Doug Risebrough, among them Mark Parrish and Darby Hendrickson. Mostly Minnesotans had just a cup of coffee with the local team—guys like Jeff Nielsen, Erik Westrum, Jeff Taffe, and the multitude of others who played only a handful of games with the Wild.

In Parise it had its first true local superstar, someone who had five times scored at least 30 goals in the NHL and once reached 45 goals and 94 points. A couple of months prior, Parise hoisted the

New Jersey Devils on his back to the Stanley Cup Final, scoring eight postseason goals in 24 games.

The name Parise carries with it decades of adoration from Minnesota hockey fans. Zach's dad, J.P., played parts of nine seasons with the Minnesota North Stars. J.P.'s pro career was over before Zach was born, but the family settled in Bloomington, where the Stars played their home games, and Zach came up through the powerful Jefferson High School youth program.

J.P. would eventually become director of hockey at Shattuck–St. Mary's School in Faribault, Minnesota. Zach and his brother, Jordan, would play bantam and high school hockey for their dad at Shattuck, and both played a role in Shattuck's 2001 national championship. From there, Zach Parise chose the University of North Dakota to continue his schooling, much to the chagrin of local hockey enthusiasts, who desperately wanted to see him take his talents to the University of Minnesota.

Parise spent two years at UND before turning professional with the Devils, the club that drafted him 17th overall in the legendary 2003 NHL Draft. The lockout then canceled the 2004–05 NHL season, delaying his debut with New Jersey until 2005–06, when he scored 32 points in 81 games.

He quickly became one of the game's most durable players early in his career, missing a total of three games in his first five years in the NHL. A knee injury wiped out all but 13 games during the 2010–11 season, but he returned to skate in all 82 in 2011–12, his final season with the Devils before signing with Minnesota.

He hasn't had the same kind of durability with the Wild, however, playing in all 48 games during the 2013 season but never skating in more than 74 games in any of his first seven seasons with the club. Still, he's scored 30 goals in a Wild uniform once while finishing with 29 one other time.

But more than what he's done on the ice, Parise has changed the course of the Wild's business operation off of it. The Wild saw its 10-year sellout streak end in 2010, and by the end of the 2011–12 season, the Xcel Energy Center routinely had plenty of empty seats for games. "We were in a tough spot," said Wild president Matt Majka. "We had struggled to make the playoffs for four or five straight years, and our roster needed serious help. The vibe around the team was low and the season-ticket base was shrinking."

Signing Parise and Suter in July of 2012 changed that, reestablishing its sellout streak as well as its waiting list for season tickets. Six consecutive playoff appearances followed.

On the sixth anniversary of his signing with the Wild, Parise opined to the *Minneapolis Star Tribune* that—no matter what happened in his career with Minnesota—signing with the club was one thing he'd never regret.

Sure, the money was great, but he was getting offers for more elsewhere. But returning to Minnesota allowed Parise to be there for his family as J.P.'s health deteriorated following a lung cancer diagnosis in 2014. J.P. lived with the disease for a year before passing away on January 7, 2015.

Suter, who had lost his father, Bob, to a heart attack just a few months prior, summed it up best. "At least the good thing is we got to be here," Suter said. "If we would have signed other places, they wouldn't have got to come to as many games as they did get a chance to come to. Looking back, that's the best thing that's happened to me."

34 Visit Tom Reid's Hockey City Pub

The landscape on West Seventh Street in downtown St. Paul was much different before the Wild and Xcel Energy Center became a reality in 2000.

Look no further than Tom Reid's Hockey City Pub, a staple on the corner of West Seventh and Walnut Street, two blocks from the Gate 2 entrance of the arena. When the NHL announced the return of hockey to Minnesota in 1997, Tom Reid's was known as Judy K's. It was one of only a couple pubs and restaurants in an area of St. Paul that had become run down in the years leading up to the announcement.

Once word got out that the NHL was coming to St. Paul, former North Stars defenseman and announcer Tom Reid got the idea to open a business as close to the arena as possible. But it was no easy task. Reid had never operated a restaurant before, so there was only a vision in his head. "I had plenty of experience on the other side of the bar," Reid said with a laugh. "This place being just two blocks from Xcel Energy Center, it was the perfect spot to be."

So Reid and a business partner purchased Judy K's in early 1999 and operated it as that for about 15 months. In June of 2000, three months before the puck drop on the Wild's inaugural season, Judy K's closed for 90 days' worth of renovations.

What was once a dark and windowless corner establishment was transformed into a hockey museum, where everything—even down to the shape of the bar—has a theme: hockey.

It opened on the night before the first Wild preseason game in franchise history in September of 2000. "We tried to open this place up," Reid said. "You can see throughout the whole bar. There aren't very many walls in here."

When you step into Tom Reid's, you can see all the way from front to back, and it invites you in. The huge windows on all sides bring in plenty of natural light during the day, allowing you to walk throughout the restaurant to scan hundreds of pieces of hockey history.

Signed items from everyone from Wayne Gretzky and Gordie Howe to Rocket Richard and Bobby Orr adorn the walls. More unique items, like signed hockey sticks and gloves from many of Reid's former teammates, are also around. You could literally spend hours just checking out all the stuff on the walls inside the bar.

New in 2018 is a giant patio that added plenty of outdoor space and some extra bathrooms to the restaurant, which is typically packed on any Wild game night—or any event night for that matter.

Stop in on an off night with the Wild in town and you're bound to run into players, coaches, or general managers from other teams, as Tom Reid's is universally known throughout the league as a must-hit when in St. Paul.

Along with other bars and restaurants, Tom Reid's has helped transform West Seventh Street from a dark, quiet road into one bustling at all hours of the day and night.

When it opened, Reid's was the third closest bar to the arena. Now, it's the seventh, a sign of how much activity has sprouted up in the two decades since Tom Reid's opened its doors. "The competition is strong, and there's more places coming all the time," Reid said. "Some of these buildings were boarded up when we came in here. There was a field next door that is now a patio. But now there's pubs going up all the time, and there are enough events down here to support every one of us. We welcome new places opening up down here because it brings more people."

35 Nick Schultz

Marian Gaborik, the first-ever draft pick by the Wild, was selected third overall in the 2000 NHL Draft.

But many people forget who was second. Defenseman Nick Schultz was selected 30 picks later out of the Canadian junior hockey ranks.

Although Gaborik is remembered for his big offensive numbers and highlight-reel goals, Schultz's time with the organization actually lasted much longer than Gaborik's.

A native of Strasbourg, Saskatchewan, Schultz made his NHL debut with the Wild in 2001, one year after being selected in the draft. Just 19 years old at the time, Schultz made the team out of training camp and put together a solid rookie campaign, scoring four goals and 10 points in 52 games that season.

Never a big scorer, Schultz made his mark in the defensive end of the rink, an area of his game deemed even more important because of the coach he played for: defensive stalwart Jacques Lemaire.

Schultz also became a favorite among fans and teammates in the locker room because of his easygoing nature and friendly demeanor.

For more than a decade, Schultz quietly went about his work in Minnesota, playing 743 games for the Wild until he was traded to the Edmonton Oilers in exchange for Tom Gilbert on February 27, 2012. At the time of the trade, Schultz had played more games in a Wild uniform than any other player.

In his time with Minnesota, Schultz never scored more than six goals in a single season. His career high in points came in 2009–10, when 19 of his 20 points came via assists.

Schultz played parts of three seasons with the Oilers before he was on the move again, when he was dealt to the Columbus Blue Jackets. He played just nine games for Columbus before signing with the Philadelphia Flyers the next summer. Schultz played parts of three seasons in the City of Brotherly Love, missing just three games in total over his first two seasons there and skating in his 1,000th NHL game on January 13, 2016.

Schultz retired from the NHL after 1,069 games, having scored 30 goals and 175 points. Not bad for a second-round pick and often forgotten man in the Wild's inaugural draft.

36 Watch a Game at Mariucci

The first of the "new" college hockey arenas in the Upper Midwest, Mariucci Arena on the campus of the University of Minnesota is a must-stop for any Wild fan that hasn't been there. For the seven years between the time the North Stars left for Dallas and the time the Wild began play in 2000, Gopher hockey was the state's most famous hockey program.

Rich in tradition, the University of Minnesota men's hockey team has won five national championships, including two since moving into its current home on campus in 1993. Prior to that, the Gophers played across the street at Williams Arena, better known as the team's basketball home. Although the hockey team played under the same roof, the ice sheet was actually at the far end of the building, where the Sports Pavilion is currently located. The team needed a more modern facility, so Mariucci Arena was built just steps away.

If you're heading there for the first time, be sure to set aside at least an hour to take a lap around the top of the single bowl seating area. Adorning the walls are photos of every team to ever play at the university, trophies the program has won, as well as Olympians to have come from the school.

Perhaps the most famous parts of the building are the large murals in the corners, boasting every All-American that has ever worn the Maroon and Gold. There are legends from all eras of the program, and the trip around the arena is like visiting a Gopher hockey museum.

Renamed 3M Arena at Mariucci in 2017, the arena has a traditional college atmosphere. If you're 90 minutes early and touring the history inside the arena, the marching band will be right along with you, playing the school's song, as well as other ear worms like "Hail Minnesota," and the "Minnesota March."

The arena is nearly 30 years old, and the school spent millions of dollars during 2016 and 2017 to modernize the bowels of the facility, bringing it up to par with other, much newer facilities and once again making 3M Arena at Mariucci one of the top college barns in the country.

37 Chuck Fletcher

If anyone was destined to become an NHL general manager, it'd have to be Chuck Fletcher. The only son of Hall of Fame GM Cliff Fletcher, Chuck had all the hands-on training one would need to break into the business when he was a teenager and his dad was running the Calgary Flames.

Born in Montreal on April 29, 1967, Chuck Fletcher knew from an early age that if he was to continue in the family business, he'd likely have to do so as a player. Cliff worked as a scout for the Montreal Canadiens, then scouted the area for the St. Louis Blues around the time Chuck was born, helping the expansion club reach the Stanley Cup Finals in each of its first three years.

Around the time Chuck was five, Cliff got his first crack at a general manager job, taking over the expansion Atlanta Flames in 1972. Over the next decade, Cliff oversaw a team that won a pair of division titles and two Presidents' Trophies, as well as a move to Calgary.

Chuck was there every step of the way, often times as a sounding board for his dad. "He was always around me in Calgary when we'd be talking about decisions that had to [be] made for the Flames back then," Cliff told ESPN in 2015.

"I wasn't a very good player so I knew if I wanted to stay in the business I had to try and follow in his footsteps or get a job in hockey," Chuck told ESPN. "I was a rink rat. I hung around, and he was pretty good letting me sit next to him during games. I used to go to morning skates, too. I knew all the players, the trainers, the scouts—it was a great way to grow up. It was a great childhood."

Fletcher graduated from Harvard in 1990 and got into hockey, first in sales for Hockey Canada, then on the player representative side with Newport Sports Management, where he worked for two years.

His big break came in 1993 when Bob Clarke hired Chuck with the expansion Florida Panthers. He survived a GM change there, working in South Florida for nearly a decade before serving as assistant GM in Anaheim from 2002–06 and in Pittsburgh from 2006–09. Then he got his first crack at an NHL GM job with the Wild in May of 2009, about a month before the Penguins won their third Stanley Cup.

In his time with Minnesota, Fletcher is often remembered for some of his misses: trading Nick Leddy, Brent Burns, and Martin Hanzal, among them. But he also made a number of moves that spurred the Wild to six consecutive postseason berths, a feat accomplished by just two other teams this decade.

It was Fletcher who set in motion the plan to sign Zach Parise and Ryan Suter, clearing cap space and making moves more than a year in advance to set the table. Fletcher traded Cal Clutterbuck for Nino Niederreiter and a third-round draft pick for Devan Dubnyk. He drafted Mikael Granlund, Jonas Brodin, Matt Dumba, and Jason Zucker among others. In his nine seasons as GM, the Wild went 359–265–80 and reached the playoffs six times, posting a sub-.500 record just one time in his tenure (35–36–11 in 2011–12). Still, the club never advanced past the second round of the playoffs, getting through round one just twice.

He was removed as GM and executive vice president of the club on April 23, 2018, after a third-consecutive first-round exit from the playoffs. The following month, he was replaced by Paul Fenton. At the time Wild owner Craig Leipold said, "My feeling is that the last couple years, we just have not been good enough. Through his strong work ethic, integrity, and vision, Chuck and his staff built a winning culture and a perennial playoff team. For all of that I am grateful."

38 Minnesota Ousts Colorado...Again

The magic and majesty of the Wild's 2014 Stanley Cup Playoff series against the Colorado Avalanche can be boiled down to Game 7.

For the third time in 11 years, the two clubs were meeting in the first round. Each of the first two times, the underdog came out on top; the expansion Wild ousted the heavily favored Avs in 2003 while Colorado eliminated Minnesota in 2008 following the club's lone Northwest Division title.

In 2014 it was Colorado—led by first-year head coach Patrick Roy—that had stormed through the NHL regular season. It's 112 points were most in the Central Division, second-most in the Western Conference, and third-most in the NHL. The Wild were the west's top wild-card team with 98 points, but the Avalanche was favored to move on.

Home teams held serve through the first four games of the series. Colorado won Games 1 and 2 at the Pepsi Center (one in overtime) and the Wild won 3 and 4 at Xcel Energy Center (also one in overtime).

Back in Denver the Avs scored an overtime win in Game 5 to take control of the series. Like in 2003, Minnesota needed consecutive wins, including one on the road, to advance.

The Wild rolled to a 5–2 win in Game 6 in St. Paul, the only game in the series truly decided by more than one goal. (Colorado's 4–2 win in Game 2 came with an empty-net tally with 15 seconds left.)

Game 7 was one that would go down as one of the most memorable games in franchise history, just like the one 11 years earlier. In one of the most unusual of stats, Colorado trailed for exactly zero

Defenseman Jared Spurgeon moves the puck against the Colorado Avalanche in Game 7 of a 2014 first-round playoff series.

seconds of game time, but lost the game—and the series—on yet another overtime heartbreaker.

The teams traded goals all night long. First it was Nick Holden of Colorado just 2:52 into the game. Mikko Koivu tied it less than six minutes later. Jamie McGinn gave the Avs the lead with six minutes left in the first period before Minnesota's Dany Heatley knotted it again 7:27 into the second. Paul Stastny put Colorado ahead for a third time at 2:55 of the third before Nino Niederreiter tied it at 6:33. Erik Johnson's goal with under nine minutes to play made it 4–3 Avs, but Jared Spurgeon tied it a fourth time with a wicked shot with 2:27 left in regulation.

Fans inside the Pepsi Center could barely catch their breath. "It was a roller coaster of a game," Wild defenseman Ryan Suter said afterward. "What a series. This group, we've got something special here."

Then 5:02 into overtime, Minnesota got the break it needed, when Heatley hit Kyle Brodziak with a head-man pass. He dished to Niederreiter, who entered the Colorado zone two-on-one. Brodziak was teed up for a one-timer, but Niederreiter fired instead, snapping a shot off the post and in past Semyon Varlamov for the series clincher. "To score a Game 7 overtime winner, it's the biggest goal you can score," Niederreiter said. "I'm very happy. I wasn't quite sure it went in, though." Indeed there was some question as to whether the puck crossed the line. Niederreiter's blazing shot went in so quick and came out so fast that Colorado's Ryan O'Reilly swooped in to clear the puck as it sat in the blue paint afterward.

The goal judge, the referee, and Brodziak were certain, however, and one look at an overhead replay confirmed it; Minnesota was moving on to the second round. The goal, which went in in the same end of the rink as Andrew Brunette's winner 11 years prior, sent Minnesota on to the second round of the playoffs for the first time since Brunette's goal in 2003.

Suter was nearly right as well. Minnesota lost in the next round to the Chicago Blackhawks, but after losing in five games to their rivals the year before, the Wild took Chicago to six games in 2014. If not for a quirky bounce off the end wall in a Game 6 loss to the Blackhawks at Xcel Energy Center, Minnesota may have had a chance at some more Game 7 magic back in the Windy City.

39 Ryan Suter

No matter what happens during Ryan Suter's tenure with the Wild, the decision to come to Minnesota was one he'll never regret.

Suter had it good in Nashville. Paired with Shea Weber, the two formed one of the NHL's top defensive pairs for a team that was on the rise in the years leading up to the summer of 2012. The Predators went to the playoffs in each of the three years prior and in six of Suter's final seven seasons in the Music City, missing the postseason only in 2009 during his entire tenure there.

Nearly every team in the league came calling on July 1, 2012, the day he became an unrestricted free agent. The Philadelphia Flyers made an offer that would have paid him well north of $100 million. The Detroit Red Wings, Pittsburgh Penguins, and the Wild were the most dogged in their pursuit of the defenseman. "I was really considering Detroit because I had known people that played there and just the way they treat their players and everything. It would have been awesome," Suter said. "I had a lot of calls, but I always kind of hinting to Zach [Parise], 'Hey, let's go back and play in Minnesota and do that whole thing.' Basically, every team reached out and all made their offer. I had offers for more money out there and I had options that would have paid more, but I felt like being in the Midwest would have been good things for me. At the end of the day, I chose Minnesota with Zach and I don't regret my decision one bit."

Suter's wife, Becky, is a native of Bloomington. In addition to the money making sense, and the opportunity to join forces with another outstanding player, it was the chance to play in front of a local audience that made it worth it.

As far as he knows, Minnesota was the only team able to offer contracts to both players that summer, so even though each took less to play for the Wild, it was the lone place where they could play together. "All the intangibles were there," Suter said. "I had always wanted to play in Minnesota. I had visited Minnesota a lot, and Becky was from there, but I also had a lot of connections. I always thought it'd be a fun place to play, the crowds were always good, I just really liked being in the Midwest and being close to home."

The Suter clan has made its home base in Madison, Wisconsin, a four-hour drive east of St. Paul on Interstate 94. For Suter, that meant a quicker drive for his dad, Bob, a defenseman on the 1980 U.S. Olympic Hockey Team, to get to more games. Ryan recalled the trips his dad would take to Nashville, driving from the family compound in Madison to Tennessee for the game before hopping back in his pickup truck and heading home. Bob wouldn't get back until the wee hours of the morning, then would head straight to Capitol Ice in the Madison suburbs and put in a full day's work. "I wanted my dad to have those close drives," Suter said, giving another reason to go to Minnesota. "He wouldn't get back until five in the morning, then go right to work."

As it turns out, the chance to spend more time with his dad ended up being invaluable after Bob passed away unexpectedly in September of 2014, as Ryan was preparing to begin his third season with the Wild. Had Ryan signed elsewhere, those two years might have been completely different.

How would history be different had Suter signed in Pittsburgh, for example? Would the Penguins have won back-to-back Stanley Cups in 2016 and 2017? Would he have a championship ring to go along with his Olympic silver medal he won in 2010?

Still, Suter believes good things are coming in Minnesota, including a chance to have the Suter name etched into Lord Stanley's Cup for the first time since 1989, when his uncle, Gary, was a member of the Calgary Flames. "We've made the playoffs and we've done a lot of good things," Suter said. "We have the potential."

During his time in Minnesota, Suter has established himself as one of the top blue liners in the NHL. An annual leader in time on ice, Suter has had a remarkable run of consistency and longevity rivaled by few others in the game today.

After he sustained a potential career-threatening injury late in the 2017–18 season, Suter worked over the summer to not only return to the ice, but to also get back before the start of the following season. "Honestly, that motivates me," Suter said. "I like doubters. When people say, 'You probably won't be ready for camp,' that just makes me angry. I might not be, but I'm sure as heck going to try as hard as I can. I'm going to be in better shape than I've ever been in. I've never worked this hard, this much."

40 It's a Jersey Thing

When Xcel Energy Center opened in downtown St. Paul in 2000, it was immediately lauded as one of the best sporting venues in the world. Even now, nearly two decades into its existence, it's still regarded by many as one of the best arenas in the NHL. Buildings in Glendale, Arizona, and Pittsburgh, Pennsylvania—among others—were modeled after Xcel Energy Center in the years after it was built.

In addition to its open-concept concourses and great sight lines, what has made Xcel Energy Center such a special building are the small details that go into making it a Minnesota building. From the décor and the colors to the smells and the names of the concession stands, everything about the building screams Minnesota.

Former Wild chairman Bob Naegele visits the Xcel Energy Center, which displays jerseys of local high school teams, a day before the stadium's debut on September 29, 2000.

One of its homiest touches came back in 2000, when former Wild CEO Jac Sperling had an idea that was unique in the sporting landscape—at least at the time. His idea was to create a tribute to the high school hockey programs around the state by displaying their jerseys above the suite level of the arena. And because the concourses were open, fans walking through the arena's Gate 1—the building's main entrance—would have an open view.

It was up to team curator Roger Godin to make the idea a reality, so he went about asking coaches of teams from around the state to donate a jersey. He then organized them and hung them up in increments—more than 200 in all—for fans entering the building to see. "Here's a non-hockey guy from New Orleans and educated in Virginia coming up with this idea," Godin said of Sperling. "It frequently takes an eye from the outside to think of something that the natives don't."

It was an immediate hit, and one of the original touches still on display at Xcel Energy Center nearly two decades after it opened. The tradition of honoring the state's high school hockey programs has special meaning in St. Paul. Each year the state's high school hockey tournaments—both the boys and the girls—are played there.

High school hockey and the city have a relationship that dates back more than five decades, so displaying the programs made sense. Before the building was erected, the boys' state tournament was traditionally played at St. Paul Civic Center, an arena that was on the site of the current Xcel Energy Center. It also started a wave of similar tributes in new stadiums around the country.

Across town, when the Minnesota Vikings moved into US Bank Stadium in 2016, it put up a high school football tribute, where teams from around the state donated a helmet that was displayed on the wall.

Even buildings built before Xcel Energy Center that didn't display high school jerseys have since added them to their arenas. Winnipeg's Bell MTS Place has a display in its main concourse honoring Manitoba high school hockey. "We can take some credit for that, not that anyone has gone out on a limb to say that," Godin said. "I know New Jersey has done it, and Columbus has done it. And I know in New Jersey's case, they talked to me directly."

41 Wild Wins the Northwest

When the Wild finished one point short of capturing its first-ever division championship in 2007, it was clear the team had that goal in mind once the puck dropped before the 2007–08 season.

The year prior, the Wild wasted a 10–2–0 start to the season and slumbered through the holidays just three games above .500. Minnesota lost just nine times over the final three months of the season but came up one point shy of the Vancouver Canucks for the top spot in the Northwest.

That one point ended up being a big one; instead of being the third seed and earning home-ice advantage in the first round, the Wild ended up the seventh seed and lost in five games to the Anaheim Ducks, the eventual Stanley Cup champion. "Last year was obviously a big step for us," Wild forward Mark Parrish told the *St. Paul Pioneer Press* in 2008. "One of our goals was to win the division last year, and we fell short. It was a little frustrating. It's tough to swallow when it's just one point."

For a second consecutive year, the Wild came out of the gates red-hot, starting the season 7–0–1. Minnesota was also far more consistent during the regular season, never losing more than three games in a row in regulation. A 4–0–1 finish to the season lifted the Wild when it needed it most, as it outpaced the Colorado Avalanche and Calgary Flames for the division title in the season's final week.

In one of the most competitive divisions in the NHL, just 10 points separated the first-place Wild from the fourth-place Canucks and Oilers, who each tied with 88 points. All five teams finished at least six games over .500. Vancouver and Edmonton finished just three points out of the eight spot, as three of the five teams in the Northwest made the postseason.

The Wild saw firsthand just how tough the division was in the first round of the playoffs, when it lost in six games to the Avalanche. Consider it a bit of payback for the Wild's upset win against the Avalanche some five years prior.

Still, Minnesota was able to witness its first NHL divisional championship since the North Stars won the Norris Division title in 1983–84. As of the conclusion of the 2018–19 campaign, it remains the only division championship in Wild history and the lone banner hanging inside Xcel Energy Center. "There will be a reminder there forever," Parrish said. "We'll be able to see that we were a part of it for as long as this building is standing, and it's real, real good to be a part of."

42 The Nick Leddy Trade

In one of his first major trades as general manager of the Wild, Chuck Fletcher took a chance on a highly drafted defenseman from the Chicago Blackhawks and in exchange dealt a first-round pick and local product that's had a solid NHL career. Needless to say, the deal didn't work out for the Wild, and in looking back at Fletcher's tenure as general manager, it's one of his biggest disappointments.

Shortly before an Olympic roster freeze, the Wild traded veteran defensemen Kim Johnsson and prospect Nick Leddy to the Windy City for defenseman Cam Barker. The third overall pick in the 2004 NHL Draft (behind Alex Ovechkin and Evgeni Malkin), Barker had shown glimpses in his time with the

Blackhawks; as a 22-year-old, Barker posted a 40-point season in just 68 games in 2008–09. But the following season, Barker came back to earth, scoring four goals and 14 points in 51 games. Buried behind Duncan Keith, Brian Campbell, and Niklas Hjalmarsson, he couldn't seem to gain any traction in Chicago, which made him expendable. The Blackhawks and Wild were not yet in the same division, so a move to Minnesota wasn't yet difficult to make.

Johnsson was in the final year of his contract and dealt with concussion issues that made him a constant question mark. One of the top puck-moving blue liners in the league when healthy, Johnsson had never been able to match some of the 40-plus-point seasons he had earlier in his career with Philadelphia. Almost 34 years old at the time of the deal, Johnsson would retire from the NHL at the end of the season, so his loss wasn't a big one for Minnesota.

Instead, it was the inclusion of Leddy, the Wild's first-round draft pick in the 2009 NHL Draft, that would bite Minnesota. "This is not a reflection on Nick at all in the sense that we didn't feel he was going to be a good player, or we didn't feel he had value," Fletcher said at the time of the trade. "This says the opposite in the fact that we were able to get a player like Barker for him. The only way you trade a player like Leddy is if you're acquiring a young player back."

A native of Eden Prairie, Leddy was skating for the University of Minnesota at the time and was having a rather underwhelming season, considering his draft status. Leddy scored just three goals and had 11 points in 30 games with the Gophers that season, and some were wondering whether he had the size to develop into an every-night NHLer.

He turned pro the following summer and quickly answered those questions. In his first full season in Chicago in 2011–12, Leddy posted 37 points in 82 games, a season in which he didn't turn 21 until late in the campaign. The following year, Leddy scored six goals and 18 points in 48 games, helping Chicago to its second Stanley Cup title in four years.

Chicago got one more season out of Leddy before trading him to the New York Islanders, where he has continued his stellar play in the Eastern Conference. His missed a total of just eight games in his first five seasons with the Islanders, posting at least 10 goals and 40 points three times.

Still well shy of his 30th birthday, Leddy already has more than 600 games of NHL experience, and his offensive ability from the blue line means he'll likely have a long career in the league.

Barker, meanwhile, skated in a total of 71 games for Minnesota, scoring two goals and 12 points before moving on to the Edmonton Oilers in 2011–12 and the Vancouver Canucks in 2012–13. Following the trade to Minnesota, Barker skated in 110 more NHL games. Then he played for two clubs over five seasons in the KHL before taking his game to Switzerland in 2018.

The trade ended up being an unfortunate one for Fletcher but showed his ability to find quality defensemen early in the draft. Leddy's selection in round one in 2009 was Fletcher's first as Wild GM, and he would later go on to snag Jonas Brodin (2011) and Matt Dumba (2012) in the opening round as well.

43 Glen Sonmor

If there's one man in the history of Minnesota hockey that's done it all, it's longtime former player/coach/general manager/broadcaster/ legendary storyteller Glen Sonmor. He wasn't a Minnesotan by birth—he was born in Moose Jaw, Saskatchewan in 1929—but he would go down as one of the state's all-time great characters.

A University of Minnesota graduate and teammate of (future Gopher coach) John Mariucci with the Minneapolis Millers in 1949, it was Mariucci who enrolled him at the University, where he would go on to graduate from in 1955 after taking summer classes for six years.

Sonmor would go on to play for the Cleveland Barons and St. Louis Flyers of the American Hockey League and in 28 games for the New York Rangers before his playing career was cut short in 1955 when he took a puck to the left eye.

Not even 25 years old, Sonmor's playing career was over. And if not for a Korean family in Cleveland, his life in hockey might have been over too. "The owners of the Cleveland team were great people," Sonmor told the *Star Tribune* in 2015. "They got me a job in mortgage banking. My first assignment was collecting on delinquent loans. You would send a letter, then a stronger letter, and, finally, you had to visit the person who wasn't making the payments.

"I made my first house call, and the door was answered by a Korean lady in a shabby dress with a baby in her arms. Her husband was in the garage and gave me the darndest sob story you've ever heard. I gave him all the money in my billfold, 10 bucks, and went back to work and told my boss, 'I don't think I'm a banker.'"

Sonmor eventually returned to Minnesota and put that college degree to work, serving as Gophers freshman coach under Mariucci, a man he would go on to succeed as coach at the school in 1966. After that Sonmor was general manager and coach of the Minnesota Fighting Saints and later coached the Minnesota North Stars until alcohol cost him his job with club in 1983.

Sonmor had had a few too many beers in a Pittsburgh-area bar and was mugged in an alley on his way back to the team hotel. North Stars general manager Lou Nanne fired Sonmor but got him into treatment.

It worked, and Sonmor was sober for the last quarter of his life. He also paid it forward, serving as an Alcoholics Anonymous mentor for hundreds of area Twin Cities residents, including many prominent former players and local celebrities. "It's the thing I'm most proud of to be an example and be able to help people who have absolutely destroyed their life," Sonmor said.

"I would say those [AA] people respected him as much or more than the hockey guys he played with and coached," Mike Antonovich, who played for Sonmor with the Gophers and with the Fighting Saints, told the *St. Paul Pioneer Press*. "Glen wanted to save everybody. I think that was his mission. He wasn't going to let you fail."

Later in his career, Sonmor also spent a decade as radio analyst of Gopher hockey games.

Perhaps the man best associated with the short-lived Fighting Saints, Sonmor was general manager of both incarnations of the club and coached the team for a stretch during its inaugural season and in its final season.

In addition to the Fighting Saints, Sonmor's legendary career in Minnesota hockey spanned eight different decades, beginning in 1949 with the Millers and ending in 2011, his final season calling games on the radio for the Golden Gophers. Sonmor died December 14, 2015, at the age of 86 after battling a number of health issues during his final years.

2016 Stadium Series Game

When Craig Leipold purchased the Wild from Bob Naegele in 2008, one of his first orders of business was to bring an outdoor game to Minnesota. It is, after all, where the roots of the game in the United States began and where kids of all ages continue to grow their love of the sport at the grassroots level.

At that time, however, the only game available was the NHL's crown jewel, the Winter Classic, played every year on New Year's Day.

The problem for the Wild was that in 2008 it had little true star power. It had no Sidney Crosby or Alexander Ovechkin to help draw in a national audience. And while the setting would have been picture perfect, the Wild were—for the most part—a very average team in the late 2000s.

When Zach Parise and Ryan Suter signed with Minnesota in 2012, that narrative began to change. By the mid-2010s, the NHL had added other outdoor games. The Stadium Series contests joined the Winter Classic, giving the league anywhere from two to four outdoor games per season.

And while a flagship event was preferable, beggars can't be choosers. Leipold had planned for an outdoor game his entire tenure as team owner and in February of 2016 he got it, when the Wild hosted the Chicago Blackhawks at TCF Bank Stadium on the campus of the University of Minnesota.

The run up to the game was filled with drama for the Wild, which had fired head coach Mike Yeo eight days prior following a lackluster effort against the Boston Bruins on national television, a game which capped a miserable month of January.

Following the promotion of head coach John Torchetti, who moved four hours north to St. Paul from his head position with the team's American Hockey League affiliate in Des Moines, Minnesota went to western Canada and won its first three games under its interim coach, setting the stage for another nationally televised contest against its chief rival.

Needless to say, the Wild weren't embarrassed this time. Minnesota poured it on in a 6–1 victory, getting contributions

Nino Niederreiter celebrates his goal with Erik Haula during the National Hockey League Stadium Series game between the Chicago Blackhawks and Minnesota Wild at TCF Bank Stadium.

from all of its lines and two of its former Golden Gophers on the roster. Playing across the street from Mariucci Arena, Thomas Vanek and Erik Haula played starring roles in the win for the Wild.

Haula had one goal and two assists, and his three points matched an NHL record for points in an outdoor game. "First to get the win and the whole team to play that well and also having 50,000 people being back where it kind of all started," Haula said afterward. "It was incredible."

Vanek also scored a goal on a pretty redirection in front.

In a memorable moment after the game, Suter held his young son, Brooks, while conducting a press conference. Brooks was getting antsy in front of the large gathered media crowd and looked like he didn't want to be there.

Asked for his most memorable moment of the day and of the week, Brooks fired back with the same straight-faced honesty his dad has perfected. "The win," he said.

A huge grin immediately came across the face of Ryan, who was very proud of his son's response. "For us to be a part of it, hopefully we can be a part of more of these because it is the ultimate experience for your family," Ryan Suter said.

John Mariucci

Another product of the Eveleth, Minnesota, hockey factory, John Mariucci reached the highest level of professional hockey but is known more for his coaching acumen.

Born on May 8, 1916, Mariucci developed under the guidance of legendary coach Cliff Thompson, who famously lost just 26 times among the 569 career games he coached in.

A left-shot defenseman, Mariucci played collegiately at the University of Minnesota, where he scored 28 goals in his final season on campus (1939–40), in a span of just 18 games. Minnesota went undefeated that season and won the AAU National Championship.

His play got the attention of the Chicago Blackhawks, who signed him to his first professional contract. He played in 24 games with Chicago the following season, his first of five NHL campaigns which were interrupted by World War II.

Mariucci played in one season in the AHL before returning home in 1949, where he played for the Minneapolis Millers and St. Paul Saints, two prominent junior teams in the area.

His foray into coaching didn't take long.

In 1952, less than a year removed from his final game as a player, Mariucci took over as the head coach at his alma mater, a position he would keep for 13 seasons. In his first season, Mariucci led Minnesota—a team that had gone 13–13 the previous season—to a 23–6 mark and a spot in the national championship game. Twice in his first three seasons as coach of the Gophers, his teams reached the national championship game.

Perhaps his most enduring legacy on campus was the dogged recruiting of in-state players. Mariucci was the first coach at the university to recruit a bulk of his roster from Minnesota instead of going to Canada for his talent.

At the time, hockey's popularity in Minnesota had crested and appeared to be on the downswing. But Mariucci's belief that the state had elite talent helped spur a revival of sorts. "This is a state institution and should be represented by Minnesota boys," Mariucci said. "If they're not quite as good as some Canadians, we'll just have to work a little harder, that's all."

It was that belief that helped foster a sense of loyalty among high school players in the state and truly where the dream of one day wearing the M began. Mariucci believed that he must be involved in even the most grassroots events of growing the game in the state. He made it to rink openings and to small towns across the state for camps and coaching clinics.

He also helped many of his former players find coaching positions themselves, a group that included Herb Brooks, Bob Johnson, Lou Nanne, and Doug Woog, among many others.

In 1956 Mariucci coached the U.S. Olympic team—with 11 Minnesotans on its roster—to a silver medal and a win over the heavily favored Canadians. Eight Minnesotans were on the 1960 Olympic gold medal team, dubbed "The Forgotten Miracle," and 12 Minnesotans, led by the head coach Brooks, were on the 1980 "Miracle on Ice" team.

Nearly all of those players and each of those medals is in some way linked to Mariucci, who earned the nickname, "The Godfather of Minnesota Hockey."

It is because of his stalwart belief in Minnesota hockey that it became a national leader in producing the best and the most talent in the United States.

A charter member of the U.S. Hockey Hall of Fame, Mariucci was inducted into the Hockey Hall of Fame in Toronto in 1985. The university renamed the hockey portion of Williams Arena after him in 1985, a name that remained on a new Gophers' hockey facility that opened across the street in 1993.

The Tourney

There's one tournament hockey fans in Minnesota take more seriously than any other in the game today: the Minnesota State High School League boys' hockey tournament, hosted each March in downtown St. Paul.

Attendance at the tournament is among the highest of all events in the nearly 20-year history of Xcel Energy Center, the host of the tournament since 2001. The three highest attended hockey games in the building's history are all high school games, including the record for any event, when 21,609 fans attended the 2015 Class AA semifinal games. That record still stands as the largest to ever watch an indoor hockey game in the state.

Most high school sports in Minnesota have some sort of state tournament, but the boys' hockey is far and away the most prestigious and historical.

It began in its current form in 1945, when athletic director Gene Aldrich organized a tournament with eight teams from around the state to play in a three-day event at St. Paul Auditorium. The eight teams were organized into regions representing all corners of Minnesota, including Rochester (Region 1), White Bear Lake (Region 2), Granite Falls (Region 3), St. Paul Washington (Region 4), St. Cloud Tech (Region 5), Staples (Region 6), Eveleth (Region 7), and Thief River Falls (Region 8), a tournament won by Eveleth.

Gate receipts from the first state tournament showed an attendance of more than 8,400 people, which allowed Aldrich to reimburse his financial backers as well as the teams for their expenses in getting to and staying in St. Paul. By the end of the weekend, the tournament turned a profit of $135.06, all of which was donated to the high school league.

Because it was profitable, the tournament returned for Year Two in 1946 and has been back every year since. Attendance the following year went over 11,000 people, and as more schools around the state adopted hockey as an official sport, the tournaments became far more competitive and tight.

For 46 years the state tournament was a one-class affair, and the top eight teams competed in St. Paul for a single state championship. Private schools, like St. Paul's Hill-Murray and Cretin-Derham Hall, were finally allowed into the tournament in 1975. The two-class state tournament began in 1994, and the largest schools by enrollment competed in Class AA and smaller schools in Class A. Teams in Class A are allowed to play up to the AA level, and several traditional powers over the years have done just that. Seeded tournaments began in 2007, with coaches from participating teams ranking the eight schools and seeding them 1–5. Teams 6–8 in each class are determined by a draw.

A tournament that began with attendances under 10,000 now routinely sees four-day event totals surpassing 120,000 each season, and many of the fans are repeat customers who have traveled in from around the state to watch regardless of who is participating. State tournament attendance for many families is an annual tradition no different than a reunion.

Mike Modano

A little more than a year after being selected by the Minnesota North Stars with the first overall pick in the 1988 NHL Entry Draft, Mike Modano walked into Bloomington's Met Center ready to begin an illustrious career that would go down as one of the best in hockey history. "I remember driving to the game that day to the Met and walking down that back ramp into the locker room," Modano told the *St. Paul Pioneer Press* in 2014. "So many games and so many scenarios, but that walk is still so vivid, like coming into that room and seeing your name in the stall and taking the ice for pregame warm-up."

It was quite the first impression Modano left on the State of Hockey; he scored one goal and assisted on another in a North Stars win over the New York Islanders.

The North Stars badly needed Modano to be a star. After Minnesota selected Brian Lawton with the first overall pick in the 1983 draft, a decision that would go down in infamy, the Hartford Whalers selected Slyvain Turgeon second, and the New York Islanders and Detroit Red Wings next picked Pat LaFontaine and Steve Yzerman, respectively.

Attendance at the Met Center was beginning to sag, and the team hadn't been beyond the first round of the playoffs in four years. The season prior to Modano's drafting, the North Stars bottomed out, finishing with a 19–48–13 record.

After the disaster that was the selection of Lawton, comparatively speaking anyway, hockey fans in Minnesota were hopeful things would be different this time around. As the 1988 draft approached, Modano and Trevor Linden were the consensus favorites to be picked atop the draft.

And while Linden would end up being a fantastic NHLer in his own right, playing in more than 1,300 games in his NHL career, Modano would go on to become the highest scoring American-born player in league history. "He had one thing that I didn't think Linden had: He was electrifying," former North Stars general manager Lou Nanne told ESPN. "He brought people out of their seats. We wanted that at that time. We thought he would be a great player. But when you draft a kid at 18, you don't think he'll be a Hall of Famer. He's the greatest American-born forward to play the game and has won a Stanley Cup and has energized two franchises. That's pretty special."

In 1,499 career games, Modano scored 561 goals and 813 assists for 1,374 points, 507 more than Linden in only 117 more games.

As it turned out, the North Stars would have struggled to have a true miss in the draft that year; seven of the top 10 picks each played at least 1,000 games in the NHL, including players like Modano, Linden, Jeremy Roenick, Rod Brind'Amour, and Teemu Selanne.

But the Michigan-born Modano gave the North Stars a quiet, shy kid with Midwest sensibilities, a player to build around for the next two decades.

In theory.

As it turned out, Modano spent just four years in Minnesota, moving to Dallas in 1993 following a 33-goal, 93-point season that would go down as one of Modano's finest. The next year, the club's first in Dallas, Modano had his only 50-goal campaign and matched the 93 points from the season prior.

Modano would never reach even 40 goals in a single season again but would surpass 30 goals six times and 20 an additional five times. He tallied at least 80 points in seven seasons after the team moved to the Lone Star State and played in seven NHL All-Star Games, helping the Stars to a Stanley Cup championship with seven points in a six-game Cup-clinching series in 1999.

He was everything those fans in Minnesota could have dreamed about that first night back in October of 1989 and so much more. Despite his short stay in the state, Modano has credited the area with helping him grow as an 18-year-old kid into a young man who would go on to become one of the best players in league history. "My time there was pretty influential because it's where it all started," Modano said. "There is always a part of my heart that will be dear to fans in Minnesota and the whole state. It was pivotal to me, the support I got at 18 moving into the city and the embrace I got from people there. There were a lot of firsts for me there."

On May 23, 2019, Modano was officially welcomed back to Minnesota by the Wild when he was named an executive adviser, a role on the business side that was nearly a year in the making. With four kids all under the age of five, Modano said he was eager to return to the state and raise his family in the place where his own professional career began.

His new role with the Wild is one those closest to him thought he would be a natural at. Lou Nanne, who drafted Modano with the first overall pick in the 1988 NHL Draft, said: "He's got something that really makes people want to be around him, enjoy being around him, and make them feel good about it."

48 Hockey Day Minnesota

It's one thing to see Hockey Day Minnesota on television. It's another to see it in person.

While the whole event comes off to some as a contrived infomercial, a complaint heard often, the pageantry of Hockey Day Minnesota is completely different for the communities that host it. Years of bidding and planning go into the event, while the hard work of local volunteers and leaders in hockey communities around the state spend hundreds of hours in an effort to simply get a chance to host the event. That doesn't even count the hundreds more hours it takes to pull off the event itself, a production that is like few others.

Although outdoor games at the NHL level have become watered down simply because the sheer number of them every season has taken a bit of the prestige away from the Winter Classic, the high school and college level outdoor games—with the tremendous production values of NHL games—are quite remarkable.

Consider the 2018 version of Hockey Day Minnesota, which was played at Lake George in St. Cloud. The refrigerated ice sheet, just steps from the lake, was in perfect condition. On the Saturday of the event, the sheet played host to a pair of high school games between ranked teams and for the first time a college game between a pair of in-state WCHA rivals. Across town the festivities continued with a men's college game at the Herb Brooks National Hockey Center. After that game, 90 minutes down the road, the Wild finished off the day with a win over the Tampa Bay Lightning.

Three sites, two cities, and one memorable day for all involved. "It was amazing the whole time. Even if you're up or down, it's just fun to be out here and playing outdoors," said St. Cloud State women's captain Brittney Anderson. "This doesn't happen often when it's this competitive and you get this many fans. It was honestly the best experience hockey-wise for me."

Those that become regular followers of Hockey Day Minnesota get to see a cross section of the state from a hockey perspective. Since the first two years of the event, which were each held on Baudette Bay, the location has changed each season, offering followers a chance to spend time in the metro Twin Cities, as well as out-of-state spots like Grand Rapids, Duluth, and Moorhead.

You're also guaranteed a first-rate hockey experience, thanks to the events of Hockey Day Minnesota 2012, which was scheduled to take place on Lake Minnetonka. Warm temperatures and thin ice on the lake forced the events of the day inside.

Every year since, the event—run in partnership with the Wild and Fox Sports North—has required communities to have refrigerated ice. And every year the event seems to get bigger and better.

49 Go to a Bulldogs Game in Duluth

Although the University of Minnesota's flagship campus in Minneapolis has the longest and most storied history of any college hockey team in the state, the recent success of its sister school in Duluth has put it on a similar level.

With three national championships since 2011, the University of Minnesota-Duluth has won more championships than its big-school counterparts while also boasting arguably the finest collegiate arena in the state.

For their first 50 years as a program, the Bulldogs were an afterthought on a local and national level. Especially with the success of the Golden Gophers during the John Mariucci and Herb Brooks eras, UMD—the state's only other Division I option for hockey at the time—was not on a level plain.

That began to change in the 1980s. Brooks was gone to the NHL, and though Minnesota still had successes, UMD began cranking out NHL talent in its own right.

The Bulldogs made the NCAA tournament for the first time in 1983, the first of three consecutive trips to the tournament. It was during this time that future Hall of Famer Brett Hull spent two years at the school.

In 1984 UMD lost in the national championship game to Bowling Green late in the fourth overtime. The following year, it lost in overtime again at the Frozen Four, this time in the semifinals.

The Bulldogs went to one NCAA tournament during the next 19 years, a span that included three additional teams in the state forming Division I programs and the University of Minnesota winning two national championships.

A region final win against the Gophers in 2004 sent UMD back to the Frozen Four and provided the university with one of its most heralded wins to date, but it wasn't until more recently that the Bulldogs became a true national power.

Beginning in 2009, the Bulldogs made the NCAA tournament in eight of the next 11 seasons, capturing its first national championship in 2011 at Xcel Energy Center in St. Paul with an overtime win over Michigan.

UMD won another title in St. Paul in 2018, knocking off Notre Dame 2–1 in the championship game for its second title under head coach Scott Sandelin. In 2019 it became the first school in more than a decade to win back-to-back NCAA titles.

In addition to its recent success, AMSOIL Arena, on the shores of Lake Superior, provides the Bulldogs with one of the finest arenas in the country. With incredible sight lines throughout, there isn't a bad seat in the building.

The city of Duluth is also one of the hidden gems in the state of Minnesota. The entirety of its downtown is within walking distance of the arena, so a variety of restaurants and bars are steps away.

A stop at legendary Grandma's Saloon and Grill in Canal Park is a must for any first trip to Duluth. Or Fill up a growler at Fitger's Brewhouse if craft beer is your thing.

If you take a trip Duluth early in the season, check out the incredible sights along the North Shore as the leaves change colors. World class fishing and golf are also not far if you want to make a weekend out of it.

50 Minnesota Miracle

Minnesota played a starring role in what is arguably the greatest accomplishment in the history of sports, the U.S. men's Olympic hockey team going on its improbable run to win the gold medal at the 1980 Winter Olympic Games in Lake Placid, New York.

Sports served as a great distraction for American citizens during that time. Embroiled in the Cold War with the Soviet Union, the U.S. was dealing with rising gas prices and record inflation at home, while international events like the Iran hostage crisis brought American confidence to an all-time low.

With the Olympics on home soil, few gave the American men much of a shot to even medal, much less win the gold.

In order to do so, the U.S. would have to get through the best hockey team in the world, the Soviet Union, which had won gold at four-straight Olympics and had dismantled several NHL teams and an NHL All-Star team during its run up to the games.

In an exhibition against the U.S. only a few days before the Olympics, the Soviets ran up a 10–3 win at Madison Square Garden in New York City.

To be certain, the United States didn't even have its best collection of talent. Coach Herb Brooks went with a hodgepodge of players—mostly from the University of Minnesota and Boston University—in an eclectic mix of personalities that he hoped would execute his vision of skating with the Soviets and eventually beating them at their own game.

In all, 12 of the 20 players on the team in Lake Placid hailed from Minnesota, as did head coach Brooks and all five support staff. It's oldest player, Buzz Schneider, was a native of Babbitt and played for Brooks with the Golden Gophers, as did Mike Ramsey, the team's youngest player, who hailed from Minneapolis.

Unlike more recent Olympics, where NHL players or professionals have taken part, each member of Team USA was an amateur player with some level of college experience.

Some, like team captain Mike Eruzione, had exhausted their college eligibility. Others, like Neal Broten of Roseau, put their college careers on hold. As it turned out, Broten was the only player who would return to the college game the following year. Every other player either turned professional or left the game altogether.

Among those with Minnesota ties included goaltender Steve Janaszak (White Bear Lake), Bill Baker (Grand Rapids), Dave Christian (Warroad), Ramsey, Broten, Steve Christoff (Richfield), John Harrington (Virginia), Rob McClanahan (St. Paul), Mark Pavelich (Eveleth), Schneider, Eric Strobel (Rochester), and Phil Verchota (Duluth). Christian is the only Minnesota native who played college hockey outside of the state, playing for the Fighting Sioux just across the border at the University of North Dakota. Pavelich and Harrington played at Minnesota-Duluth.

In addition to St. Paul's Brooks, the team also had manager Ralph Jasinski (Mounds View), goalie coach Warren Strelow (Mahtomedi), Dr. George Nagobads (Edina), trainer Gary Smith (Minneapolis), and equipment manager Bud Kessel (St. Paul), all with Minnesota roots.

The team was inducted into the U.S. Hockey Hall of Fame in Eveleth in 2003, where it occupies a large area inside the museum as a tribute to its accomplishments. The gold medal in Lake Placid is credited with increased American participation and interest in hockey, a sport that at the professional level was once dominated by Canadian-born players.

51 Mike Yeo

When Mike Yeo was hired as the third head coach in team history, his arrival came as a bit of a surprise.

The team's general manager at the time, Chuck Fletcher, was two years into the job and was already hiring his second head coach. First, it was Minnesota native Todd Richards returning home after one season as an assistant with the San Jose Sharks.

The Richards experiment went south, as he finished outside the playoffs in both years as coach, prompting Fletcher to make another move. Richards, who was 44 when he was dismissed, had been a head coach in the minors, but the gig with the Wild was his first as the top NHL coach.

During the summer of 2011, it was widely believed the Wild would hire an experienced retread head coach to lead a team that had missed the playoffs three consecutive seasons and had not advanced past the first round of the postseason in eight years.

Ken Hitchcock, Michel Therrien, and Craig MacTavish were potential candidates to replace Richards, along with Yeo, who had just finished up his first season as the head coach of the Wild's AHL affiliate in Houston.

In the end the familiarity with Yeo—who Fletcher had worked with when both were with the Pittsburgh Penguins organization—won out over experience. "At the end of the day, the only good reason that I could come up with why Mike shouldn't be the coach was because he was 37 years old," Fletcher said. "The longer I watched Houston play, it just became more apparent the longer the process went that Mike was the guy. Their attention to detail and the way they played night in and night out and knowing what I was looking for in a coach."

The day he was hired, Yeo was the same age as Andrew Brunette and John Madden, two players who were among the club's leading scorers the year before. Yeo had six years of playing experience in professional hockey, including five years with the Houston Aeros when they were in the IHL. He posted solid offensive numbers in his playing days but was better known for his rough-and-tumble demeanor.

Yeo also captained the Aeros to the Turner Cup championship in 1999 before embarking on a coaching career that led him to Wilkes-Barre/Scranton and eventually Pittsburgh as an assistant before heading back to Houston. "I always felt that I was going to be a coach. I knew that was a passion that I had inside of me," Yeo said. "The experience I was able to get by jumping in headfirst and forcing myself into these situations, I knew that I was ready."

In Yeo's first season, the Wild were the best team in the NHL around Christmastime, an anomaly that quickly corrected itself; Minnesota finished 14 points out of a playoff spot and in 12th place in the Western Conference.

The following summer, the Wild brought in prospect Mikael Granlund and signed forward Zach Parise and defenseman Ryan Suter to long-term contracts, changing the face of the organization forever and changing the expectations for Yeo overnight. "The reason we're all sitting here is we want to win a Stanley Cup," Yeo said at the press conference introducing Suter and Parise on July 9, 2012. "It's much more excitement instead of pressure."

A lockout that wiped out half the following season delayed the debut of Parise and Suter in Wild uniforms, but the club overcame a another late-season swoon to reach the playoffs on the final day of the 2012–13 season.

Unfortunately for Yeo, the annual Wild swoon became as much a part of his lore in Minnesota as the consecutive playoff appearances. The Wild made the postseason in each of the next three seasons, typically overcoming a multi-week post-holiday downswing. Minnesota even advanced in the playoffs twice, the first time since 2003 it had accomplished that feat.

But it was the swoon that would eventually cut Yeo's time short with the club, as he was fired February 13, 2016, after a 4–2 loss to the Boston Bruins where it was clear the team had given up on its embattled head coach. Minnesota posted a 3–12–4 record in Yeo's final 19 games as coach of the team. Its 10 points during that stretch represented the fewest in the NHL.

"I'm a realist," Yeo said a few days before he was removed as head coach. "You can't lose every game and expect to think that there's not going to be changes." At the time of his firing, the Wild were 11th in the Western Conference. Its 0–5–3 record in his last eight home games was Minnesota's longest winless streak on home ice in 15 years.

Unlike the previous season, when a 2–8–4 run prompted Fletcher to trade for goaltender Devan Dubnyk, there simply wasn't a trade out there to save Yeo's job.

The club named Iowa head coach John Torchetti as Yeo's interim replacement, and the Wild rallied to make the playoffs for a fourth consecutive season but lost in the first round once again, prompting Fletcher to hire the experienced Bruce Boudreau in the summer of 2016 as the fourth full-time head coach in club history.

52 Visit the U.S. Hockey Hall of Fame

Many cities wanted the distinction, but only one—tiny Eveleth, Minnesota, three hours north of the Twin Cities—was given the honor of becoming the host of the United States Hockey Hall of Fame.

By the early 1970s, the U.S. was becoming more of a player on the international scene in hockey. A gold medal in the 1960 Olympics was the first for the country, but more and more Americans were playing the game at the highest level than at any point in history. With the NHL expanding to markets like Pittsburgh, Philadelphia, Los Angeles, St. Louis, and Minneapolis in 1967, participation in the game was expected to dramatically increase.

Dedicated in 1973, the U.S. Hockey Hall of Fame and Museum was placed in Eveleth for one main reason: more members of the Hall were from the city than any other city or town in the United States. Thanks to an unparalleled history with the game that dated back six decades, Eveleth became the home for the country's greatest shrine to hockey.

Located just off U.S. Highway 53, a stone's throw from the world's largest hockey stick (another landmark definitely worth your time if you find yourself in the area), admission to the U.S. Hockey Hall of Fame is more than reasonable; a family of four can get into the museum for a total of $30 or less.

Once inside, the Hall boasts an unrivaled number of jerseys, photos, autographed items, videos, and more, all planned and placed in a way that tells the story of American hockey. The building stretches more than three stories in height. Each level showcases a new league or a new group of teams.

Not surprisingly, the 1980 Olympic team plays a big role inside the museum. For anyone fascinated by the events in Lake Placid and the Miracle on Ice, visiting the Hall is a must-stop.

The same goes for anyone interested in learning about the legendary Minnesota State High School League tournament. Jerseys, team photos, tourney programs, and video testimonials of legendary high school teams from the past adorn the walls of the museum in one of the country's great showcases of prep sports.

Save time to visit the hockey stick, located a mile or two away in the heart of downtown, a park that is walking distance from the famous Eveleth Hippodrome. Inside the Hipp is another museum paying homage to Eveleth teams of the past.

Walter Bush

Few figures in the history of the sport have had a bigger impact on hockey than Minneapolis' own Walter Bush.

Bush learned to play the game as a child of the Depression, skating for a military school and for Dartmouth University in New Hampshire before moving back to Minnesota to attend law school.

He played in the United States Hockcy League before beginning a remarkable career off the ice that spanned six decades. In the 1950s Bush served as president of the newly minted Central Hockey League before becoming a member of the board of directors of the Amateur Hockey Association of the United States, which would eventually become USA Hockey.

He served as a team manager of the 1960 U.S. Olympic Hockey team, "The Forgotten Miracle" that went on to win a gold medal over the heavily favored Soviet Union team. After the Olympics, Bush served as president of the Minnesota Amateur Hockey Association from 1961–63 and ran the CHL's Minneapolis Bruins from 1963–65 until setting out on perhaps his most ambitious journey yet: bringing the National Hockey League to Minnesota.

Bush successfully lobbied the NHL for a team, and in 1966 Minnesota was awarded the North Stars, a franchise that Bush would lead as president for 10 seasons and for two more as chairman of the board.

As 1980 approached, Bush was again tasked with helping the United States find a way to end the Soviets' grip on the gold medal. Alongside fellow Minnesotan Herb Brooks, and a number of Minnesota-born players, Bush was an integral part of helping the 1980 "Miracle on Ice" Olympic team stun the sports world by winning gold in Lake Placid, New York.

That same year, Bush was elected to the U.S. Hockey Hall of Fame.

Beginning in 1986, Bush served 17 years as president of the AHAUS until his retirement in 2003. During that span, Bush was instrumental in the growth of the women's game, including its inclusion as an Olympic sport for the first time in 1998. For his efforts, Bush was awarded the Olympic Order from the International Olympic Committee, the highest honor awarded by the Olympic movement.

Until his death in September of 2016, Bush served as chairman of the board of USA Hockey. He was elected to the Hockey Hall of Fame in Toronto in 2000. In a state filled with towering figures of the sport, few stand taller than Bush.

Wild Finds the Win Column

October 18, 2000, dawned with the expansion Wild sitting winless in its first five games. Minnesota opened its first-ever regular season on the West Coast, losing 3–1 to the Mighty Ducks of Anaheim and 4–1 to the Phoenix Coyotes on back-to-back nights.

A 3–3 tie against the Philadelphia Flyers in the first game at Xcel Energy Center gave the Wild its first point, but two more losses—one at St. Louis and the other at home to Edmonton—left the Wild at 0–4–1 through its first five games.

It wasn't as though Minnesota wasn't competitive early, however. The Wild trailed Anaheim by one goal almost midway through the third period but couldn't find the equalizer.

Minnesota scored the game's first goal 24 hours later in Phoenix, playing from in front for the first time. After its tie against the Flyers, the Wild and Blues were scoreless deep into the second period, a trend that would continue for much of the season; the Wild finished as the 12th stingiest team in the league despite its status as an expansion club.

Minnesota led through a bulk of the first period and a half against Edmonton but saw its lead slip away late in the second period on goals by veterans Ryan Smyth and Doug Weight.

Back at home, the Wild desperately needed to find the win column. An opportunity against the struggling Tampa Bay Lightning provided it with a chance to do just that, but an early goal by Vincent Lecavalier put the Wild behind just seven minutes into the game.

The Wild came alive in the second period, thanks for Maxim Sushinsky. The Russian forward was one of Minnesota's best players over the first couple weeks of the season, and he scored twice, while also assisting on another goal—all in the second—as Minnesota turned a 2–1 deficit into a 4–2 lead after two periods.

Now 20 minutes away from its first win, the Wild simply needed to shut things down. Todd Warriner got Tampa Bay within one 3:47 into the third period with a short-handed goal, one that sapped Minnesota's chance to put the game away.

When Alexander Kharitonov tied the game almost 10 minutes later, it appeared Minnesota was about to give away yet another game.

But as the clock winded down, it was the team's first superstar, rookie sniper Marian Gaborik, that got the Wild back on track. His third goal of the season with 2:28 left in regulation sent Xcel

Jamie McLennan, Lubomir Sekeras, and Sean O'Donnell congratulate Marian Gaborik, top center, after their 6–5 win against the Tampa Bay Lightning on October 18, 2000, for the first win in franchise history.

Energy Center into a frenzy. He added an empty-net goal with 58 seconds left to put the game on ice.

Gaborik's bonus goal ended up as the winner as Tampa scored a goal with 12 seconds left. But for the Lightning, it was too little, too late.

For the first time since April 10, 1993, when the North Stars defeated the Blues 4–3 at the Met Center, Minnesota fans watched their NHL team win a game on home ice. The victory was the first of 25 wins in the Wild's first season in the league.

55 Billy Rob

Of the hundreds of people who have left their imprint on the Wild over its first two decades in the franchise, few have had as much wide-ranging and day-to-day impact as Bill Robertson.

One of the first dozen employees brought in by Bob Naegele, Robertson served as the team's first public relations maven and eventually become the club's vice president for communications and broadcasting.

In addition to his everyday duties once the team began playing games, Robertson played a big role in the years after the franchise was announced but before it started playing games. Robertson, known around Xcel Energy Center as "Billy Rob," was no stranger to helping expansion teams get off the ground. He worked for the Minnesota Timberwolves as the NBA franchise across town got its start. He also worked for the Anaheim Mighty Ducks and Anaheim Angels (before they were the Los Angeles Angels). He was on board as the Ducks franchise started and worked on the complete rebranding of the Angels.

Unlike previous stops, where Robertson began jobs with teams a few weeks or months before the inaugural season began, he spent more than two years laying the groundwork for the Wild before it ever played a game. "I said, 'Why do you want a communications and broadcast person here two and a half years before you play a game?'" Robertson remembered asking Jac Sperling. "And he said, simply put, 'You are the guy who can get us all this publicity and good will. No one else can do that.' Instead of taking out ads and paying to put things out, they used [me]."

During that time Robertson was tasked with keeping the Wild on the front burner of the sports landscape, even though it wasn't garnering any headlines with games.

No idea was a bad idea. And with plenty of time to spare before the Wild hit the ice, Robertson and his crew got to work. "Some days, I felt like P.T. Barnum," Robertson said. "They were looking for me to create stunts. When you have the time to think about stuff and actually sit around and drum up ideas, that's a good thing."

One of his favorites came late in the process, when the arena needed to host a sort of soft opening in order to test the plumbing. Instead of having workers shuffle out and participate, Robertson had an idea to invite a bunch of area youth hockey teams to come participate in what he called, the "super flush." Local television crews showed up in droves and followed the kids around the arena as they went about flushing toilets. With its catchy title, "super flush" even made the Howard Stern radio show.

Robertson chuckled just thinking about it. "Bob Naegele came into my office one day in the summer about three or four months before the first game and said, 'Hey, Billy, wouldn't it be great if we never had to play a game and we could just keep doing this?'" Robertson said. "It was the greatest line ever, and I still use that one. But I told him I knew exactly what he meant because there were no wins and losses. Everything we did turned out really well.

There wasn't a lot of mistakes made. We hired really exceptional people, and I give Bob and Jac a ton of credit for seeing and hiring the right people."

A St. Paul native, who attended high school at Cretin, the opportunity to come home and work for a professional sports franchise was a dream come true.

Minneapolis had dominated the pro sports landscape in Minnesota from the time the Twins and Vikings moved from suburban Bloomington to the Hubert H. Humphrey Metrodome in 1982. St. Paul tried to get into the pro sports game, pitching itself as a potential home for the Twins during the 1990s. The legendary St. Paul Civic Center, which hosted the Minnesota Fighting Saints of the World Hockey Association in the 1970s, was an option for NHL teams interested in relocation after the North Stars left for Dallas in 1993. But with just 15,000 seats and lacking modern amenities, it was quickly dismissed.

But under the leadership of then St. Paul mayor Norm Coleman, the city partnered with Naegele and the state of Minnesota to build what would become Xcel Energy Center, bringing the smaller of the two Twin Cities into the pro sports marketplace for good.

As a proud St. Paul guy, Robertson beams just thinking about it. "The electricity level outside the arena before our first regular season game was like nothing I've ever experienced before in my professional life," Robertson said. "It had a lot to do with me being a St. Paul native and seeing St. Paul being transformed. My first four months on the job, I was living in executive apartments in Lowertown and I would walk toward our offices. At 5:00 you could roll a bowling ball through the skyway. It was a little unique. When the Wild played its first-ever exhibition game, downtown St. Paul changed instantly. It was just totally different; restaurants, bars, hotels, energy level…it was magical."

North Stars Become Lone Stars

Two decades after joining the National Hockey League as part of the league's expansion of 1967, the Minnesota North Stars appeared to be on their last legs.

The club had reached just one Stanley Cup Final in its history, and by 1989, attendance and support for the team had dwindled, thanks to several noncompetitive seasons.

Team owners George and Gordon Gund desperately wanted to move the team to the San Francisco Bay Area, something the NHL did not want. The league liked Minnesota's hockey-crazed market and believed it could work out if only a couple of things could happen.

So, in a move rarely seen today, the NHL allowed the Gunds to trade ownership of the North Stars franchise for an expansion team that would be placed in San Jose and become the Sharks. Howard Baldwin and Morris Belzberg took over ownership of the North Stars on August 9, 1990. The two would later bring in Norm Green, one of the original owners of the Calgary Flames, as a partner. Green soon purchased controlling interest in the team, and it was his job to revive fledgling interest in the hockey club.

Once one of the finest buildings in the NHL, the Met Center was in need of renovations. When Green arrived he put money into the arena—but not as much as he originally wanted. Following the North Stars' trip to the 1991 Stanley Cup Finals, a series they lost in six games to the Pittsburgh Penguins, Green unveiled a plan to put more than $30 million into the building, along with an adjacent shopping mall.

Those plans fell through, and although Green did make some minor cosmetic changes to the building, the Stars' future in Minnesota was all but settled. Green first tried to move the franchise west, to Anaheim, California, where he had a deal to make the club the L.A. Stars. But the NHL nixed that deal when Disney offered to kickstart an expansion franchise there and put the strength of its marketing behind it. With that the Mighty Ducks were formed—ironically, named after a youth hockey team based in Minnesota.

Because Green allowed the NHL to reenter the Southern California market with an expansion team, the league agreed to allow Green to move the franchise anywhere he could get the best deal.

In 1993 Dallas presented him with just that: a chance to start fresh and eventually with a new arena. "In our first year, the new fans were rewarded by the success on the ice and in the playoffs," Green wrote in an article for *DMagazine*. "Many of the fans were knowledgeable in hockey, having moved here from northern hockey communities. Others were just excited to see the action of a new, fast contact sport and often responded to action on the ice at the wrong time. We quickly knew we had made the right decision, as our attendance and average ticket price were more than double what we received in Minnesota."

The NHL lockout of 1994 raised player salaries and eventually forced Green to sell the team to Dallas businessman Tom Hicks. The Stars went on to win their first Stanley Cup in franchise history in 1999, then moved into American Airlines Center in 2001.

Hockey has thrived in north Texas ever since. "In 1993 there was only one poor sheet of ice at Valley Ranch," Green wrote. "Now there are almost 30 in the area, with tens of thousands of young people playing hockey and participating in skating programs. I look back with incredible pride at the decision to bring the NHL to Dallas."

57 Aronson Makes History

When Marian Gaborik was drafted out of Slovakia with the third overall pick in the 2000 NHL Entry Draft, he made history by becoming the first-ever player drafted by the Wild. He was not, however, the first player on the Wild's roster. That honor belonged to Steve Aronson, who became the first player to sign a professional contract with the Wild after completing a standout four-year college career at Division III University of St. Thomas, a few miles down the road from Xcel Energy Center.

Aronson, a native of Minnetonka, Minnesota, was a three-time First-Team All-American for the Tommies and was named the Division III National Player of the Year following the 1999–2000 season. "It wasn't the path people normally took," Aronson said. "I went [to St. Thomas] to learn."

When he completed his college career, he had scored more points than any player in the history of the Minnesota Intercollegiate Athletic Conference. Three times Aronson scored at least 57 points in a season at St. Thomas, averaging nearly two points per game as a junior, when he scored 23 goals and had 60 points in 31 games and nearly three points per game as a senior, when he scored 36 goals and 86 points in 31 games.

When he won D-III National Player of the Year honors, he became the first player from the MIAC to do so. "Steve is the finest player that I've ever coached, bar none," said Terry Skrypek, Aronson's coach at St. Thomas, who carved out a career in coaching that spanned nearly four decades.

Aronson's journey to the Wild began during his historic senior season. It wasn't long before scouts from several teams were regularly in attendance, but it was a chance meeting with Wild scout

Glen Sonmor that helped launch his tenure with the club. Sonmor, the legendary former coach of the Gophers and the North Stars, made the four-hour drive from the Twin Cities to Stevens Point, Wisconsin, to watch Aronson play in a game.

Aronson finished the game with 14 penalty minutes, including a pair of double minors and a spearing penalty. "Not a good look," Aronson said with a laugh. "My coach was like, 'Glen is here, he wants to meet you.' And I just looked at him and said, 'Ugh, really?' I felt bad, and [Skrypek] said, 'Don't worry about that with Glen.'"

Fortunately for Aronson, his resumé spoke for itself. At the conclusion of the hockey season, he charged local agent Neil Sheehy to take care of matters while he joined the St. Thomas baseball team in Fort Myers, Florida.

Once they returned to Minnesota, Sheehy let Aronson know that then-Wild general manager Doug Risebrough was interested. The two met for dinner, and then Risebrough brought Aronson to the not-yet-finished new arena. Days later, despite more appealing financial offers from other teams, Aronson made history as the first player for the Wild. "It's pretty tough to pass up," Aronson said. "I didn't grow up wanting to be a Wild player, but I grew up wanting to be a North Star. And to have that opportunity, I felt was a great one and I took it."

Aronson joined a select list of players from the league to sign a contract with a National Hockey League team. While some MIAC players have been drafted through the years (none in the last two decades) and others have played minor league hockey, it's believed just one has played in an NHL game: Bob Paradise, a St. Mary's University grad who went on to play for the Pittsburgh Penguins, Atlanta Flames, Washington Capitals, and Minnesota North Stars.

It didn't take long for Aronson to have an aha moment in the league. In the Wild's second preseason game against the Mighty Ducks of Anaheim, he found himself on the ice at the same time as Paul Kariya and Teemu Selanne. During the game Selanne caught

Aronson up high with his stick, opening a cut under his eyebrow that needed stitches.

Aronson never played a game in the NHL, but he did carve out a two-year pro career in the AHL, IHL, and ECHL as well as overseas in Britain before embarking on a coaching career that brought him back to his old stomping grounds, first as an assistant for two years at St. Thomas and then back to Minnetonka High School, where he's been for the last decade.

In 2018 Aronson helped his old high school to a state championship at the Minnesota State High School League boys' hockey tournament in St. Paul, the school's first-ever state championship. "I'm super grateful that I was able to play at the highest level and that someone took the chance to sign me," Aronson said. "I'll always be really thankful to be able to test myself against the best in the world. I always wish I would have played better and had a little bit more. But when you look back, I'm happy about that chance. I had a $100 suit from Men's Wearhouse that I had worn a few times in college and then all of the sudden I was on a chartered plane with stitches from Teemu Selanne. That was pretty cool."

58 Watch a Game in Mankato

The bulk of Minnesota's prestigious hockey history lies from the Twin Cities of Minneapolis and St. Paul north to the Canadian border, where the sport has its grips on the state for five or six months every year. But there is a burgeoning hockey powerhouse in the southern part of the state as well, as Minnesota State University in Mankato continues its ascent in the NCAA.

A longtime power in the Division II and III ranks—like its sister school in Bemidji—the Mavericks have only been a Division I team for two decades. Only recently has coach Mike Hastings turned MSU into one of the most formidable teams in the country. Since his hiring in 2012 through the end of the 2018–19 season, no Division I team in America won more games than the Mavericks.

Where that success hasn't translated is at the NCAA tournament level, where MSU is still in search of its first-ever win in the big tournament. Once that success comes, there's little holding the school back from becoming a top-tier national program.

That's in large part because of the commitment of the school to make an investment in the program, including its home arena, the Mankato Civic Center. With its purple seats, revamped ice system, and overhead scoreboard, it's a much different facility than it was during the first decade of the 2000s, when Golden Gopher fans would pack the building half full in maroon and gold every time the University of Minnesota would travel south.

With the Gophers now in a different conference and the Mavericks' success on the ice, locals have come to support their team largely in spite of whichever opponent is in town.

Watching a game in Mankato provides hockey-loving families with a great option that won't clear out a bank account—it's only a short drive south of the Twin Cities, but its ticket prices reflect its place outside of the metro area.

In addition to a winning team on the ice and a mostly full arena, fans that check out Mankato for the first time will stumble upon a program that has produced some pretty good players over the years, most notably, David Backes of the Boston Bruins. Backes pumped more than $100,000 into the arena's renovations to create a state-of-the-art weight room.

A night out in Mankato is also an affordable option with plenty of dinner and beverage opportunities within a short walk of the arena. If you make it to town, some of the best pizza in Minnesota is at Pagliai's in downtown, a short walk from the arena. Pub 500 and Blue Bricks are also hockey-centric spots to grab dinner and some drinks, each of which is in the heart of downtown Mankato and won't be overloaded with loud, obnoxious music and over-served college students.

59 The Stanchion Game

During its run of six consecutive playoff berths from 2013–18, the Wild has never advanced past the second round of the postseason, not only because it's been clearly outplayed, but also because it's had its share of bad luck.

Perhaps its worst came during the second round of the 2014 Stanley Cup Playoffs against the defending Cup champs, the Chicago Blackhawks. It was the second of three consecutive postseason meetings between the new division rivals. During the lockout-shortened season the year prior, the Wild were outclassed in the first round, sneaking into the playoffs as an eight seed before being bulldozed in five games by Chicago, which went on to claim the championship.

In 2014, however, the Wild showed considerably more pluck. After dropping the first two games of the series at United Center, Minnesota rallied for a pair of wins at Xcel Energy Center to tie the series at 2–2. Back in Chicago for Game 5, the Wild secured a 1–0 lead late in the first period on a goal by Erik Haula. But the Blackhawks rallied with a second-period power play goal by Bryan Bickell and a third-period tally by Jonathan Toews to escape with a 2–1 victory.

Another low-scoring game took place in St. Paul in Game 6. Kris Versteeg scored 1:58 into the game to give the Blackhawks the early advantage. Haula tied it 2:29 into the second, and the teams played a scoreless third, going to overtime for the first time in the series.

Playing on home ice, Minnesota certainly didn't get a home-town hop in the extra session. Almost midway through the first overtime, a Blackhawks defenseman sent a routine shot in into the Wild zone. But instead of rimming around the boards, the puck hit a stanchion and bounced right back into the slot.

Goaltender Ilya Bryzgalov remained in the crease but was clearly surprised by the turn of events. Blackhawks forward Peter Regin had the first crack at it but was outmuscled by Wild defenseman Ryan Suter, who rode him off into the corner.

Minnesota's issue was the second guy on the scene: Blackhawks sniper Patrick Kane. Already off balance from the weird carom, Bryzgalov was teetering after Regin failed to get a shot off. With the puck even more to his right now, the goaltender used his left skate to push himself in that direction. Kane won a race to the loose puck with Wild forward Matt Cooke, saw Bryzgalov moving, and moved the puck swiftly to his backhand. With an entire net to shoot at, Kane tucked a shot under the crossbar for the game winner and the series clincher.

"It's an empty feeling when stuff like that happens," Wild captain Mikko Koivu said after the game. "They got that bounce, and there's absolutely nothing we can do about that play." Minnesota outshot Chicago 35–27 in the game and went toe-to-toe with the Blackhawks all series long, only to see its hopes of advancing to the west finals sniffed out by a tough bounce.

The clubs met in the second round again the following year, but the Blackhawks swept Minnesota in four games en route to another Stanley Cup championship.

In three subsequent trips to the playoffs after that, the Wild were eliminated in the first round each year. To this day, the 2014 series remains Minnesota's best chance of advancing to the third round since 2003. "It's tough. There's really not much to say," Wild forward Nino Niederreiter said. "It could have gone either way."

60 Bob and Tom

When the Wild moved Tom Reid from the television booth to the radio broadcast in 2002, it was reuniting a pair of classic voices from Minnesota winters past.

Some 30 years prior, Reid and Bob Kurtz began their partnership on television, broadcasting North Stars games for local television.

At the time, Reid was a few years removed from a playing career cut short by a skin condition known as "gunk." The rare ailment essentially made Reid allergic to his hockey equipment, and the only relief from it was to quit playing.

A native of Fort Erie, Ontario, who played long before the days of million-dollar contracts, Reid was forced into early retirement.

But he wasn't away from the game long. Within two years, he was back in the broadcast booth, working with legendary North Stars voice Al Shaver calling North Stars radio broadcasts. "I didn't have a job, I didn't expect to retire, and we didn't make a lot of money in those days," Reid said.

Two years later, Walter Bush, then president of the North Stars, asked Reid if he'd have interest in going onto the television side and working with Kurtz. Inexperienced and terrified of the new challenge, Reid went to a local TV studio and interviewed for the job, doing a mock broadcast with Kurtz.

Reid ended up getting the gig. "I asked them, 'How are you going to train me?'" Reid said. "And they said, 'You'll learn on the job.' And that's what I did. All of a sudden, I'm wearing the earpiece and people are talking. Nobody had ever told me people would be talking when I was trying to talk. But I learned."

Reid credited his time with Shaver for his successful transition into broadcasting. He spent 10 years with the North Stars before moving on when the team was sold to Norm Green in 1990. He then worked with Frank Mazzocco on University of Minnesota hockey broadcasts for a decade until the Wild came into existence in 2000.

After two years on television with the Wild, the team asked Reid if he'd be open for a reunion with Kurtz, reuniting a duo that had worked games for a handful of years nearly 20 years earlier. "I wasn't enjoying the TV as much," Reid said about the change back to radio.

The partnership extends beyond just the radio airwaves, however, as Kurtz and Reid are good friends away from the rink. The two have hiked the Grand Canyon together and gone on trips to Alaska with their families.

It's a partnership that is evident when you hear them make a radio call. "We have a pretty good feel for each other, when I can come in, because I don't want to step on his call," Reid said. "There's only two of us, just Bob and I. We don't have statisticians, we don't have camera guys, we just have our eyes, and they have to tell the story. They have 37 people, and we have two, and Bob doesn't miss too much. He's one of the best in the business, and it's been great working with him."

61

Willard Ikola

It's tough to say which part of Willard Ikola's hockey career was the most successful. Another in the long line of legendary net-minders from "Goalietown USA," Eveleth, Minnesota, Ikola was born in 1932 and idolized a number of famed goaltenders from his hometown. Frank Brimsek, Mike Karakas, and Sam LoPresti were all heroes of Ikola; all were also natives of Eveleth and each is enshrined in the U.S. Hockey Hall of Fame.

By the time Ikola was between the posts for the Eveleth Golden Bears as a freshman in 1947, the future Hall of Famer was leading his team to the state championship. Over the next three seasons, Ikola backstopped Eveleth to three consecutive undefeated state championships.

After finishing his career in his hometown, Ikola went on to the University of Michigan, where he was a three-year starter for the Wolverines. Twice he led Michigan to the national championship, including in 1953, when it defeated the University of Minnesota in the title game.

The Wolverines were upset in Ikola's senior season, falling in the national semifinals in an upset loss to RPI—finishing two wins shy of another championship three-peat.

Unlike the legendary Eveleth goaltenders before him, Ikola never played in the NHL. He served in the military and played on the 1956 U.S. Olympic team before retiring as a player and returning to Minnesota.

His association with the game was far from over, however. Just two years after playing in the Olympics, Golden Gophers coach John Mariucci (another Eveleth native) convinced Edina High

School to hire Ikola as its hockey coach. He was brought on on a trial basis and went 4–9–5 in his first season with the school. Luckily, Edina had faith in Ikola, who would never post another losing season in his coaching career, one that spanned more than three decades.

Over his 33 seasons as head coach of the Hornets, Ikola—and his famous houndstooth hat—would post a 600–140–38 record, leading Edina to eight state championships. In addition, Ikola helped construct one of the most formidable youth systems in the state, helping keep the Hornets among the state's elite long after his retirement from coaching in 1991.

Edina High School remains one of Minnesota's preeminent powers in high school hockey, both on the boys' and girls' sides. Their home facility, Braemar Arena, is one of the very best in the state in terms of both quality and access.

Hornets' boys' teams have won five more state championships since Ikola's retirement with the girls' team winning three, creating a tradition of prep hockey excellence rivaled by few in Minnesota.

62 2016 Stadium Series Alumni Game

For the first time in 25 years, fans in Minnesota looked onto an NHL sheet of ice and saw the famous green and gold sweaters of the Minnesota North Stars flapping in the breeze.

The Wild's Stadium Series game in February of 2016 was a long time coming for the newer of Minnesota's two NHL teams, and many traditionalists never thought they'd see the legendary North Stars' sweater on the ice again.

As part of the Stadium Series weekend at TCF Bank Stadium in Minneapolis, the NHL planned an alumni game between the Chicago Blackhawks and a "Team Minnesota," a group comprised of former North Stars and Wild players.

On that night, they skated together in the color of the North Stars, paying homage to the current NHL club by putting a Wild logo patch on the left shoulder. While the green and gold jerseys were worn for the first in nearly three decades, former North Star Lou Nanne, who served as a coach for the Minnesota alumni team, admitted it was likely a one-time thing.

That's what made the experience for so many older fans among the 37,922 in attendance wax nostalgic—and for Nanne too. "It might not seem like anything," Nanne said afterward, "But as I told them before the game, 'This is the last game we're going to play against the Blackhawks. We're not losing this game.'"

Some players were better prepared than others. Mike Modano, the North Stars' first overall pick in the 1988 NHL Draft, looked like he could still play. So did former Wild forward Wes Walz, who was on the ice every day as a high school hockey coach in the area.

Not surprisingly, even some of the senior alumni stepped up their game, especially in the heat of the moment. "When that game started going, even though guys can't skate, guys were yelling from the bench," Nanne said. "It was that little extra push because you wanted to end up winning the game." For others, there was plenty of personal pride on the line.

The marquee event of the weekend was the Wild and Blackhawks game scheduled at the stadium the following day. Players from the active roster, especially those who grew up in Minnesota, took time during the alumni game to watch members of the Wild's coaching or development staff.

Andrew Brunette, who scored the legendary Game 7 goal to eliminate the Colorado Avalanche during the 2003 playoffs, skated in the alumni game and served as an assistant coach on the bench for the Wild the next day. Darby Hendrickson played in the alumni game, and the Wild assistant coach was the team's "eye in the sky" the following afternoon. Richard Park and Brad Bombardir skated with the old-timers and had prominent front-office roles. All of this created an interesting dynamic for current Wild players used to hearing it from their coaches.

For others, it was one final chance to skate and feel those competitive juices flow one final time in front of a large home crowd. "A lot of times for us hockey players after we retire the lights go off and don't come on for a long time," Walz said. "Some guys struggle with that throughout their retirement. So for the lights to come back on for three or four more hours; for a lot of us, that was a lot of fun."

63 Mikael Granlund

Hockey is a big deal in Minnesota, but for Mikael Granlund, the sport had made him a cultural sensation back in his home country of Finland. Before signing his first contract with the Wild in the spring of 2012, Granlund was like a rock star back home. One year prior, Granlund's lacrosse-style goal against Russia at the world championships is a major reason for his rock star status.

With the game scoreless early in the second period, Granlund won a puck battle in the right corner of his offensive zone, skated around a defenseman under the goal line, and scooped the puck on his tape, stuffing it under the crossbar at the left post. The goal quickly went viral, and in the early days of Twitter, it was replayed over and over.

Up until that point, perhaps the best-known lacrosse goal came off the stick of Mike Legg of the University of Michigan, one that helped knock the University of Minnesota out of the NCAA tournament in 1996. It was a goal that dashed the hearts of hockey fans throughout the state.

This time Granlund's goal gave fans hope that one of the world's best young hockey players would one day put on a Wild uniform. Signing in Minnesota also gave Granlund, a first-round draft pick of the Wild in 2010, the gift of anonymity.

Quiet and reserved in public, the spotlight had become a little much for Granlund back home. Paparazzi had followed him around for the two years prior to his signing. "I think it will be, to some extent, a relief," Todd Diamond, Granlund's agent when he signed, told the *St. Paul Pioneer Press*. "In some ways he can be a little bit like Lennon and McCartney walking over there."

Granlund announced his signing with the Wild in May of 2012 in a video that remains one of the most watched in the history of the team's website. His arrival was just the first in a major roster upheaval for Minnesota that off-season. Less than two months later, the club signed Zach Parise and Ryan Suter to matching 13-year, $98 million contracts.

The adjustment to the North American game wasn't easy for Granlund, however. He skated in just 27 games with Minnesota during the lockout-shortened 2012–13 campaign, scoring two goals and eight points. Granlund scored a combined 16 goals over a 131-game span the following two years before bumping that total up to 13 in 2015–16, the first time he played a full 82-game schedule.

He broke out in his fifth season, scoring 26 goals and 69 points after moving to the wing full time. He spent the first part of his career at center, and the move to right wing allowed him to focus less on the defensive aspects of his game and more on being the creative playmaker he was during his developmental years in Finland.

He followed up his 26-goal campaign with his second 20-plus goal season in 2017–18 despite battling injuries early in the year, showing the move was no fluke.

The Granlund era in Minnesota came to a close early in 2019 when he was traded to the Nashville Predators for Kevin Fiala, ending the tenure of one of the franchise's most popular players.

64 Not a Bad Consolation Prize

With its first season in the books, the Wild embarked on the summer of 2001 with big plans. The lowest scoring team in the NHL by a wide margin in its inaugural season, Minnesota lit the lamp just 168 times in 82 games during the 2000–01 season, an average of just 2.05 goals per game.

Its dearth of offense ended up being a hindrance to its bottom line; the Wild allowed only 210 goals (12th best in the NHL that season) but still finished with 68 points in the standings, the second fewest in the Western Conference.

General manager Doug Risebrough was excited about the young and talented Marian Gaborik, the franchise's first-ever draft pick the previous year and someone who scored a team-leading 18 goals as an 18-year-old in the NHL.

But Minnesota needed more. Risebrough and his staff wanted some star power, and Alexander Mogilny was an unrestricted free agent. Mogilny, the Russian star who had scored 43 goals with the New Jersey Devils the season before, had apparently narrowed his final choice down to two teams: Minnesota and Toronto.

After some hemming and hawing, Mogilny ended up signing with the Maple Leafs. (Risebrough did not confirm on the record that Mogilny was the player Minnesota pursued, but it has been confirmed by a secondary source with direct knowledge.) Risebrough informed his staff that the player they wanted was indeed signing in Toronto. For them, it was back to the drawing board. "I remember walking into the room with all the scouts and everything, and I said, 'He's not coming, we need to start looking at somebody else,'" Risebrough said. "And their heads all hung down."

In a search for another impact player, Risebrough made a suggestion. "What about this Brunette guy?" he remembered asking his staff, which included assistant general manager Tom Lynn.

Opinions trickled in; he was the smartest player one scout had ever coached. Another brought up his lack of foot speed. But Lynn said Risebrough had already built a team loaded with speed. After listening to everyone's thoughts, the GM was sold, and the Wild inked Brunette to a four-year contract.

The rest, as they say, is history.

65 Herb Brooks

When people outside of Minnesota think of Herb Brooks, they see the character portrayed by Kurt Russell in the Disney movie, *Miracle*.

Russell's portrayal of Brooks, even down to the thick Minnesota accent, is as close to spot on as you can get in a Disney movie. Of course, the company took some creative liberties in some of the speeches Brooks gave to his 1980 Miracle on Ice team.

But for so many in Minnesota, Brooks was far more than just the coach of the 1980 Olympic Men's Hockey team. He helped resurrect the state's flagship college hockey program, turning a last-place team into a three-time national champion in the span of less than a decade. He assisted in the start of another Division I program within in the state, a landmark accomplishment credited with helping to make Minnesota five deep in D-I hockey programs. Brooks was, until the day that he died, an ambassador for the game—and for hockey in the state—because he believed it was his duty to make sure the sport was in a better place when he was gone than it was when he arrived.

A proud native of the east side of St. Paul, Brooks played high school hockey at St. Paul Johnson, leading the Governors to the state championship in 1955. He played at the University of Minnesota under coach John Mariucci, before going on to play for a number of Olympic and U.S. national teams during the 1960s.

And while his playing career is often underrated, it was his coaching career—which began back at the U in 1972—that truly established Brooks' iconic status. After losing in the NCAA championship game in 1971, the Gophers fell to 8–24–0 during the 1971–72 season. Brooks was hired as head coach and immediately sparked a seven-win improvement in 1972–73.

In year two, Brooks won the Western Collegiate Hockey Association's Coach of the Year award, leading the Gophers to a 22–11–6 mark and the first NCAA championship in program history.

But he wasn't done. Minnesota lost in the NCAA title game in 1975 but returned again in 1976, getting to the championship for the third consecutive year. Like its first trip under Brooks, the Golden Gophers defeated Michigan Tech University 6–4 for its second title in three years.

After a down season in 1977, Brooks and the Gophers laid the foundation for perhaps his best team yet at Minnesota. They went 22–14–2 in 1977–78, setting the table for his swan song with his alma mater. The Gophers won their third national championship

Herb Brooks, who coached the Miracle on Ice team to a goal medal, looks on from the bench during the closing minutes of the semifinal game against the USSR at the 1980 Olympics.

in 1979, posting a 4–3 win over rival North Dakota, capping a 32–11–1 season, the most victories Brooks had during his seven-year run as Gophers coach.

"We went to the finals four of my seven years there, and we made a great run of it," Brooks told Ross Bernstein in the book *Remembering Herbie: Celebrating the Life and Times of Hockey Legend Herb Brooks.* "I think I put a lot of pressure on the players, and I had a lot of expectations of them. I didn't give them an 'out,' and I think I was always able to find the kids who were really competitive. The common denominator of all the guys who played throughout my seven years was that they were really competitive, very hungry, very focused, and mentally tough—to go along with whatever talent they had. I think that really carried us."

After the 1979 season, Brooks was offered the impossible job of coaching the 1980 U.S. Olympic team, a squad tasked with defending home ice in Lake Placid, New York. The Americans were a long shot to even medal. The Soviet Union was heavily favored to win gold a fifth consecutive time. Sweden, Finland, Czechoslovakia, and Canada also iced teams good enough to compete for a medal.

More than the Olympics itself, it was the year-long run up to the games that cemented Brooks' legacy. It began when Brooks insisted the U.S. change the way it played the game in the first place. "Our style of play was probably different than anything in North America," Brooks told Bernstein. "We adopted more of a hybrid style of play—a bit of the Canadian school and a little bit of the European school. The players took to it like ducks to water and they really had a lot of fun playing it. We were a fast, creative team that played extremely disciplined without the puck."

Brooks was also able to deftly oversee a unique mix of personalities.

During a heated matchup in the 1976 NCAA semifinals, the Gophers and Boston University engaged in a nasty bench-clearing brawl less than two minutes into the game.

By 1980 tensions hadn't cooled, and the animosity portrayed in *Miracle* between guys from Minnesota and Boston was real. Somehow, Brooks was able to navigate that by making himself the single villain, uniting the players against him.

A brilliant coach, he rallied his troops in time for the 1980 Games, as the U.S. scored a goal in the final minute of his team's 2–2 tie against Sweden in their opening game. Wins over the Czechs, Norway, Romania, and West Germany followed, advancing the United States to the medal round matchup against the best team in the world.

Less than a week before the start of the games, the Soviets hammered the U.S. 10–3 in an exhibition played at Madison Square Garden.

The United States led just 10 minutes of the Olympic matchup, but it was the most important 10, as the Americans rallied three different times from one-goal deficits, taking the lead on captain Mike Eruzione with 10 minutes remaining.

A stellar effort from Jim Craig in goal helped the United States weather a late Soviet storm; the goaltender made 36 saves in all to help the U.S. spring perhaps the greatest upset in the history of sports, 4–3.

Many forget, however, that the United States did not win gold with its win against the Soviets. A victory two days later against Finland was required for that. If it had lost to Finland, it's possible the Americans wouldn't have medaled at all.

Again, the U.S. rallied from a pair of one-goal deficits, scoring three times in the third period to close out a 4–2 win. Against all odds, the Americans had earned not only a medal, but a gold one. "Throughout the Olympics, they had a great resiliency about them. I mean they came from behind six or seven times to win. They just kept on moving and working and digging," Brooks told Bernstein. "We were as good a conditioned team as there was in the world, outside maybe the Soviet Union. We got hot and lucky at the right times, and it was just an incredible experience for all of us."

Brooks would coach in the Olympics twice more in his career, leading Team France in 1998 before a return to the U.S. bench in 2002, helping the Americans to the silver medal, the country's first medal in men's ice hockey since the famed 1980 team.

In between, Brooks coached four different NHL teams and helped transition St. Cloud State University into the state of Minnesota's third Division I program. (Minnesota and Minnesota Duluth were the first two.) Since then, both Bemidji State and Minnesota State Mankato have added D-I hockey teams. "I remember there was talk of a five-year plan to go Division I," said current University of Minnesota coach Bob Motzko, a former player and coach at St. Cloud State who was there when Brooks took the SCSU job. "Herb came in. I think he did it in one year. Within one year, we were independent, plans to build a new arena and making progress to get into the WCHA. That was the power and the impact of Herb Brooks. He was legendary status."

Brooks continued his ambassadorship of the game until 2003, when he was killed tragically in an automobile accident in the Twin Cities. He was on his way home from a charity golf tournament on behalf of the U.S. Hockey Hall of Fame in Biwabik when his car went off Interstate 35 in Forest Lake, only a few minutes from getting home safely. He had celebrated his 66th birthday only a week prior.

66 Staal's 42-Goal Season

Eric Staal is a confident guy. But when he signed a three-year, $10.5 million contract with the Wild on July 1, 2016, there's no way even he could have figured his career would rebound in Minnesota the way it did.

The third overall pick in the 2003 NHL Draft, Staal was one of the league's top players through the end of his first decade.

Staal scored at least 70 points in seven of his first eight seasons in the NHL, topping 80 twice during that span and reaching 100 points once. He helped the Carolina Hurricanes, the team that drafted him, to a Stanley Cup in his second season as a 19-year-old.

That season, he scored a career best 45 goals and saw his point total jump from 31 in 81 games as a rookie the year before to 100 in year two.

A model of consistency and durability during his time with the Hurricanes, he missed just 22 games total in 12 seasons there, and 12 of those came during the 2009–10 season. He went to four All-Star Games and won an All-Star Game MVP and became a member of hockey's Triple Gold Club, earning a Stanley Cup, an Olympic Gold Medal, and gold at the world championships.

But by his last season in Carolina, the Hurricanes were one of the league's worst teams, and Staal appeared to be running out of steam.

A trade to the playoff-bound New York Rangers at the trade deadline in 2016 did nothing to revitalize his stats, and that summer, when he reached unrestricted free agency, his market appeared to be somewhat limited.

Desperately in need of a center, the Wild reached out, and new coach Bruce Boudreau assured Staal he'd be the centerpiece of his team's top offensive line.

With his hometown of Thunder Bay, Ontario, just an afternoon's drive north of the Twin Cities, Staal signed on with Minnesota. "It's been a lot of fun," Staal said. "I knew coming here I was joining an already very good team with some players hoping to do bigger and better things. And I was just trying to fit and be a part of it."

Within two years, Staal's career was back on track.

After a fantastic opening salvo in Minnesota, a season in which Staal again played in all 82 games and scored 28 goals and 65 points—his highest totals in more than five years—Staal was even better in year two, representing the Wild in the All-Star Game in Tampa.

Staal also surpassed the 30-goal plateau, then caught fire down the stretch reaching 40 goals for just the second time in his career. In the season finale in San Jose, Staal tied Marian Gaborik's franchise record with 42 goals during the regular season.

Perhaps more importantly, Staal was back in the playoffs consistently after being a part of some dreadful Hurricanes teams during the latter portion of his tenure there. "I feel like I've been motivated ever since I've tried to make it to the NHL. I've always been extremely competitive," Staal said. "But there's definitely a little bit added there just because of how tough those last couple years [in Carolina and New York] were mentally, and there was a lot of behind-the-scenes stuff that people don't know you deal with at home with hockey and life. So there was a lot of motivation to try and find success, and it's been a good fit. But I still want to prove there's a lot more left."

Perhaps more important that getting back on track was how Staal went about doing it. A respected captain in the Hurricanes dressing room, Staal didn't wear a permanent letter with the Wild.

Mikko Koivu, Zach Parise, and Ryan Suter were long-established locker room leaders when Staal arrived.

Instead, he went about his business in a lead-by-example manner. It quickly earned the respect of his teammates and Boudreau, the coach so instrumental in bringing him to Minnesota in the first place. "He comes to play every night. You need that No. 1 center," Boudreau said. "He does it, it seems, like every second night with different wingers. And he never complains. He just goes out there and plays. He's a real professional. That's the one thing I've gotten from knowing him."

67 Minnesotans Infiltrate the NHL

When it comes to producing NHL-caliber hockey players, no country in the world has done it as well as Canada.

According to the website HockeyReference.com, Canadian provinces far outpace the rest of the world in producing the planet's best hockey players. Prior to the 2019–20 season, the province of Ontario had produced an astounding 2,304 players in the NHL's 100-plus year history—far more than any other enclave in the world.

Quebec (825), Alberta (591), and Saskatchewan (511) were the next most, while Manitoba (389) and British Columbia (389) lagged behind even more.

By the same measure, the United States had produced 1,250 NHL players, with nearly 22 percent of those players coming from the state of Minnesota. Through the end of the 2018–19 season, Minnesota's 271 NHL players produced ranked more than the country of Finland (215) and just behind the combined Russian total of 284.

No other state in the U.S. had produced more than 200 NHLers. Massachusetts comes in at 198 and Michigan's 177 ranks third. New York (125) is the only other state with at least 69 players to reach the NHL.

As the American influence in the NHL has grown over the years, so has Minnesota's contribution. "I've traveled around the world watching kids play, and there is nothing like Minnesota," said New York Islanders scout Trent Klatt, an in-state product himself. "You can't go any place in the world and watch 16-, 17-, 18-year-old kids playing for their communities like this. This is awesome. This is better than the NHL…It's hockey in its purest form."

During the 2017–18 season, 57 Minnesotans skated in at least one NHL game, far more than any other state. Those players each came from varying backgrounds. According to Minnesota Hockey, 53 of those 57 played high school hockey in the state at some point during their career, and 31 of them finished their senior seasons with their local prep team.

As the NCAA's reach into the NHL has grown, again, so has Minnesota's influence. All five of Minnesota's Division I college teams were represented in the NHL. Around the country 196 Minnesotans played Division I hockey during the 2018–19 season.

68 1991 Cup Run

When the Stanley Cup Playoffs began in 1991, not much was expected from the Minnesota North Stars.

The fourth-place finishers in the Norris Division, the North Stars would not have come close to even making the playoffs in today's NHL. At the time there were just 10 teams in the Campbell Conference, eight of which made the playoffs.

The structure of those playoffs was even more unique: the top four teams from each division made the playoffs, regardless of record or points. Similar to the NHL's current divisional structure (minus the wild-card teams), the fourth-place team in each division played the first-place team, while the second and third-place clubs dueled in the other series. The winners of each would play in the second round or the division championship series.

In 1991 Minnesota finished 27–39–14, good for just 68 points. But because the Toronto Maple Leafs—the Campbell Conference's worst team—was also in the Norris, it was the North Stars who earned a date and, a seemingly quick playoff exit, against the Chicago Blackhawks in the first round.

Chicago finished the regular season as the NHL's Presidents' Trophy winners, posting a 49–23–8 record and a league-best 106 points.

After overcoming a Chicago goal 13 seconds into Game 1 to earn a win in overtime, the North Stars gained a bit of confidence. Two consecutive losses put Minnesota behind in the series, but the team rallied, salvaging a 3–1 win on home ice in Game 4 before a shocking 6–0 rout of the Blackhawks at Chicago Stadium.

The loss had to have stunned the Blackhawks, who couldn't rally in Game 6 back in Bloomington as Minnesota closed out the series with another 3–1 win. In doing so, the North Stars became the first team in two decades to eliminate the NHL's regular-season champion in the first round.

But the task got no easier in round two, as the North Stars faced the St. Louis Blues in the Norris Division finals. St. Louis finished the regular season one point behind Chicago in the standings and was the second-best team in the NHL.

As they had in the Blackhawks series, the Stars scored a Game 1 win to grab early control as well as home-ice advantage, something

Minnesota was able to maintain throughout the series. Following a win by the Blues in Game 2, the North Stars won both Games 3 and 4 at the Met Center to take a commanding 3–1 series lead.

St. Louis extended the series in Game 5, but the North Stars closed out the Blues on home ice with a 3–2 win in Game 6 at the Met Center.

At this point, it was clear something special was happening. "Our power play found this groove, and teams could not play against us the way they had previously because we just cut them off with our power play," North Stars coach Bob Gainey told the *St. Paul Pioneer Press* in 2015. "That's what happened to us that year."

Minnesota followed a similar recipe against Mark Messier and the defending Stanley Cup champion Edmonton Oilers in the Campbell Conference Finals, scoring a Game 1 victory and holding serve at Met Center, taking a 3–1 lead back to Northlands Coliseum in Game 5.

This time, the North Stars closed things out, advancing to the Stanley Cup Finals for the first time since 1981.

It was there where Minnesota's dreams of securing its first Stanley Cup would die, however. Minnesota won Game 1 on the road to take the lead in the series. It also won Game 3 to maintain home ice to that point, putting itself two victories away from a championship. But the Penguins took control of the series in Game 4, scoring 19 goals over the next three games, including eight in an 8–0 series-clinching win at Met Center in Game 6.

The North Stars came up short in their unlikely quest for a championship but ignited a passion for pro hockey not seen in the state in more than a decade. It made it all the more painful when the team packed and left for Dallas just two years later. "It was a brief window of maybe seven weeks with a lot of intensity," Gainey said. "And the interest went from zero to 60 real quick and it got super intense and fun."

69 Watch a Game in Las Vegas

In terms of a national following, the Wild aren't on the same level as the Chicago Blackhawks, the Montreal Canadiens, or pretty much any other Original Six franchise.

But for a team that entered the league in 2000, the number of Wild fans that pack opposing arenas is pretty good. That's especially true in a place like T-Mobile Arena in Las Vegas.

Think about it: what better way to get away from a frigid winter than to escape to the sun and warmth of Vegas for a few days? Flights from the Twin Cities are typically very affordable (MSP has two airlines that fly direct to LAS, so competition is fierce.) A hotel room at a resort on the Strip is what you make of it. Fans that want the true Vegas experience can spend a little more, while the more budget conscious can certainly find those options as well.

Perhaps the most difficult part of road tripping for a game in Vegas is finding a ticket to the packed T-Mobile Arena, though that wasn't a problem for Minnesota's first trip to the building in March of 2018.

In one of the most impressive showings by visiting fans all season, Wild fans packed the stands in Las Vegas—and the bars just steps outside the arena—watching Minnesota score a 4–2 win in the first-ever game between the teams in Nevada. "Our crowd from Minnesota was absolutely fabulous, and it made for one loud building," said Wild coach Bruce Boudreau after that game. "If you can't play in this atmosphere with that going on, I think we'd be in trouble."

Impressively, the Wild were one of just two teams to win each of its games against the Golden Knights during the expansion team's historic inaugural season, which saw Vegas advance to the Stanley Cup Finals. Minnesota was the only team to win three games against the Knights. (The New York Islanders won each of two meetings.)

Hockey fans in Minnesota have gained a reputation around North America as being some of the most knowledgeable and passionate in the NHL. Wild fans aren't afraid to applaud and appreciate some of the more obscure things they witness, things that fans in many other markets may not pick up on. It's a very old-school, traditional market.

That's not the case in Las Vegas, and fans making the trek better be ready to have fun and make a lot of noise. It'd be easy to compare a crowd at T-Mobile Arena to that of a college game, but that wouldn't be giving the Vegas crowd enough credit. Alex Ovechkin of the Washington Capitals said it was more like a party, and Boudreau, after his first trip into the building, said, "It was like a rock concert out there. I've never been involved in something where, the visiting crowd, there was so many of them. I couldn't believe how many people made the trip."

During every break in the action, the large overhead scoreboard encourages and interacts with fans in the stands, which means there is almost a constant buzz in the building. The acoustics inside T-Mobile Arena, which hosts some of the biggest musical acts in the world, are exemplary. The lighting is state of the art.

The best part for any fan visiting from the chilly north? You can come to the game in shorts and flip-flops. Leave the parka at home. When you walk out of the arena postgame, it's a comfortable—and short—walk to all kinds of world-class entertainment.

The Vegas experience is like no other in the NHL and makes one wonder why it took so long for the league to discover it.

70 Andrew Brunette

Andrew Brunette knew from the time he was a kid skating on the outdoor rinks of Valley East, Ontario, that speed would never be his forte.

Brunette remembers being about 11 years old when his coach told him about the doubts others would have about him as he grew older. "He told me, 'You're gonna get knocked for this and that. But don't let people tell you what you can't do, believe what you can do,'" Brunette said. "And I was kind of like, 'What are you talking about?' I was young, I had just scored a lot of goals, and I was like, 'Yeah, whatever, what is he talking about.' Sure enough, a couple of years later, I got cut for my skating. I knew young that I was not the fleetest of foot."

Luckily for Brunette, he played in an era of the NHL when speed wasn't everything. But don't confuse that lack of speed with being a bad skater. Indeed, he was never a 200-foot powerhouse when it came to his skating, but below the faceoff circles in the offensive zone and in the dirty areas close to the goal, few were better. "Below the bottom of the circles to the goal line in the offensive zone, I would say I've never seen a player as dominant as Andrew Brunette was any time he'd get the puck down there. I loved playing with him," said former Wild forward and teammate Wes Walz. "I just loved getting the puck to him down by the goal line because I knew if he spun away from somebody, there was going to be a good chance that he'd make a good play with it."

Brunette honed those skills in Valley East, a small town just north of Sudbury. While he played plenty of youth hockey on outdoor rinks and at Centennial Arena in town, Brunette credits the hours upon hours of street hockey he played in honing those

During the third period of a 2008 game against the St. Louis Blues, Andrew Brunette scores his 200th career goal.

skills around the goal. "I was the youngest kid on the block for a while, and we'd play road hockey with 10 or 12 guys on a narrow street," Brunette said. "The only way to have the ball was to protect it. And you're in tight areas all the time. It's the same at the outdoor rink, when you go there and there's 50 kids. The only way you have the puck is to protect it. I was quicker in certain areas, but puck protection and my hands are what allowed me to survive the outdoor rinks and the ball hockey games playing up with the older kids."

They're also what elevated him to a long National Hockey League career, one that began with the Washington Capitals during the mid-1990s. After posting huge seasons in the Ontario Hockey League, Brunette was drafted by the Caps in the seventh round of the 1993 NHL Draft.

He turned pro the following year, and the numbers kept coming: 12 goals and 30 points in 20 games in the ECHL and nine goals and 20 points in 26 games in the AHL. Brunette scored 30 goals and 80 points in 79 games in his first full AHL season with the Portland Pirates before making his NHL debut in 1995–96 with Washington.

Over the next four years, Brunette guessed he was sent up and down between the NHL and AHL more than a dozen times, all the while putting up prodigious numbers in the American League and producing at a solid clip in Washington.

In 1998 Brunette was selected by the Nashville Predators in the expansion draft, giving him his first shot at a permanent NHL gig. He'd never again return to the American Hockey League.

After one year in the Music City, Brunette went to another expansion team, the Atlanta Thrashers. It was here where he'd have his first of six 20-goal seasons in the NHL and where he'd establish himself as a rock solid regular in the league. After two years there, it was expansion team number three, as he signed a contract with Minnesota.

Even after a 69-point season and scoring the biggest goal in franchise history, Brunette says it was his time in Washington that always provided him with the chip on his shoulder that would guide him through a career that spanned more than 1,100 games, 489 of which came in a Wild uniform.

A big part of that was a commitment to playing every night. Brunette played a full 82-game schedule seven times, played in 81 games two times, and played in 80 games once. Between 1998–99 and 2011–12, his final year in the league, Brunette missed a total of just 18 games.

All of that came as a player who did a bulk of his work in some of the game's most physical areas of the ice. "In the beginning of my career, I sat out a lot," Brunette said. "I sat out so many games and sat in the press box so much over the course of my first few years, so that when you're in, you don't really want to come out. That stuck with me my whole career."

When Brunette arrived in Minnesota, he found a roster full of guys—Walz, Jim Dowd, and Darby Hendrickson among them—who shared a similar mentality. It's what made those early Wild teams so difficult to play against on a nightly basis. "In my mind, I always thought, *Who knows when your career is going to end?*" Brunette said. "You gotta play as much as you possibly can because you know not playing is no fun. You wanted to play as much as you possibly could. It was a love of the game and not wanting to miss a moment of it because who knows when you're going to get those moments? Think about that Colorado goal. Those are the moments you work so hard for and you don't want to miss them."

71 Matt Cullen

Matt Cullen's legacy in the state of Minnesota goes far beyond the four years he's spent over two different tenures with the Wild.

Virginia, Minnesota, born and Moorhead, Minnesota, raised, Cullen is one of the finest players to come from Minnesota in the modern era, or the post–North Stars era.

Amazingly, the time between the North Stars leaving and the beginning of Cullen's NHL career isn't as wide a gap as one would assume, considering Cullen signed up for yet another season in the league during the summer of 2018—25 years after the Stars left for Dallas.

Cullen debuted in the NHL on October 28, 1997, as a member of the Mighty Ducks of Anaheim back when the team resembled the bunch from the Disney movie with the aqua and purple uniforms. He's dropped the gloves in his career twice. The last came February 14, 1999, against Jeremy Roenick.

The fact that Cullen is still playing at a high level more than two decades later is one of the finest feats in NHL history. Once Jaromir Jagr left the NHL in the middle of the 2017–18 season, Cullen assumed the role of the oldest player in the league.

It didn't take long for that news to filter into the Wild dressing room. "I saw that coming when I started seeing the news. I was like, 'Oh boy. Here we go,'" Cullen said. "I don't really know what to say. Whatever. It is what it is. I've been around for a long time."

Cullen played with Jagr for one season with the New York Rangers during the 2006–07 season, giving him a firsthand look at what he would one day need to keep playing at an advanced age.

At the time Cullen was a 10-year vet and probably thought he was closer to the end of his career than he was the beginning. Little could he have known that he was still immersed in the first half of his career. "I was so impressed with how much he puts in to taking care of himself and committing to the game," Cullen said. "That was kind of before guys were doing a lot of that. He was really committed to doing what he needed to do. He was there before everybody. His late-night workouts are pretty well documented. It takes a lot to continue to play at that age." In many ways, Cullen is the same way.

Few athletes put more of an emphasis on conditioning and being in shape than Cullen, who enjoys working out more than most. For the past several years, Cullen has gone through a will-he-or-won't-he decision regarding his hockey career, and oftentimes, the decision to play has come after he's spent some time in the gym.

Even when the day comes when Cullen won't play hockey anymore, it's likely you'll find him at the gym. "I enjoy training, which I guess is part of the reason why I've been able to play as long as I have," Cullen said. "I really enjoy that side of it, but I like trying different training methods and different things with my diet. I've been really interested in it for quite a while."

Cullen is also a deeply committed family and spiritual man, who takes both very seriously. He and his wife, Bridget, met in Moorhead. She went to Minnesota State University and played basketball while he went off to St. Cloud State University and starred for the Huskies hockey team.

Together, they have three boys, but because Cullen has played so many years in the league, he's been able to share some of his finest memories—including two Stanley Cup championships with the Pittsburgh Penguins—with his family. "I've had more experiences in the game of hockey than I could have ever dared to imagine. It's beyond anything I ever would have hoped for, a kid coming out of a small town," Cullen said. "I love the game of hockey and I always have. But I never would have imagined winning three Stanley Cups and having played as long as I have."

72 Walzie Walks Away

Wes Walz knew the end was near as 2006 turned into 2007.

Finishing up his sixth season with the Wild after a career that began in the NHL and ended with him playing four seasons in Switzerland, Walz had returned to North America when the NHL expanded by two teams in 2000.

Even though the Nashville Predators and Atlanta Thrashers had entered the league in the previous two years, and the Columbus Blue Jackets were entering the same year as the Wild, Minnesota was the only team to reach out to Walz in the early summer of 2000.

Walz had become a fan favorite in Minnesota, but because he came to the Wild as a 30-year-old forward, his prime years in the league were a thing of the past by the time 2007 rolled around.

After playing in 62 games in 2006–07, a season in which he scored nine goals and 24 points and finished a plus-3, Walz skated off the ice following a Game 5 first-round loss to the Anaheim Ducks that convinced him his career was over. "I remember skating off the ice, thinking that was gonna be the last time I'd put my skates on. I was ready to retire," Walz said. "My body was sore. I didn't like the way I was playing. Other guys were playing better than me, and to be perfectly honest, I was ready to retire that summer."

Despite his desire to walk away after the playoff loss to the Ducks, Walz was talked into coming back for another season. But it didn't take long for him to realize that he simply didn't have it anymore. "My heart was never really completely into it," Walz said. "I still trained hard and I was ready to go, but I remember coming home even after training camp and going, 'I've lost something. I don't have the speed that I had. There's something missing.' I didn't like the way I was playing, I really didn't."

Walz stuck around for the first 11 games of the 2007–08 season, scoring one goal and assisting on three others, but he was a minus-5 during that stretch. Walz hadn't been a minus player since 2000–01, the Wild's inaugural season.

Wild coach Jacques Lemaire and general manager Doug Risebrough knew Walz had been having second thoughts before the season had even commenced and told Walz to stay away from the rink for a few weeks to think about what he wanted to do.

One common misconception over the years is that Walz was unhappy with the team or with his role on the team and had issues with that he needed to work through. Walz says nothing could be further from the truth. "I wanted to make sure I did it early enough that I wasn't hurting the team later in the season," Walz said. "The Wild were unbelievable about it. Tom Lynn and Doug Risebrough were unbelievable, just giving me some time to be away from the rink to reconsider. They gave me a few weeks, but nothing really changed for me. My heart wasn't into playing anymore. I only knew how to play one way, and that was all-in. I didn't want to be 80 percent into it; I didn't feel that was fair to the organization. I didn't want to steal anybody's money. This game has been too good to me."

One month after playing in his final game in the NHL on October 30, 2007, the Wild held a press conference announcing Walz was retiring from hockey. When leaving the team, Walz had played in more games in a Wild uniform than any other player.

As far as he knows, he's the only checking center in NHL history to receive a press conference upon retirement, a fact he still gets a laugh out of. "I was telling guys, 'All you need to do is retire 10 games into a season and you get your own press conference,'" Walz said. "Otherwise all you do is ride off into the sunset at the end of the year."

Walz wasn't away from hockey long. The following season, he joined the Tampa Bay Lightning as an assistant coach. Walz said he did the right thing by ending his playing career when he did. "I didn't want to cheat the Wild. They were great to me, and I'll always have a soft spot for this organization," said Walz, now a television commentator for Wild games. "There was no feeling sorry for myself. I have no regrets."

73 Devan Dubnyk

It was a deal that raised more than a few eyebrows at the time.

It was January of 2015, and the Wild were embroiled in one of their (seemingly) annual swoons. One week prior, then-head coach Mike Yeo lit into his team in a memorable on-ice, expletive-laden meltdown before breaking his stick over the boards and leaving the ice during a team practice in St. Paul.

The Wild had lost eight of its 10 games and were sitting six games outside the playoffs. Their goaltending simply wasn't up to snuff, and the coach admitted so in a press conference after his tirade. Despite being one of the stingiest teams in the league when it came to shots against, Minnesota's goalies were near the bottom when it came to save percentage.

Instead of firing his coach, general manager Chuck Fletcher traded a third-round draft pick to the Arizona Coyotes for goaltender Devan Dubnyk.

A first-round selection of the Edmonton Oilers in the 2004 NHL Draft, Dubnyk was between the posts for some of Edmonton's leanest years. Not that there was an abundance of talent around him. The Oilers were annually one of the league's doormats during his time in Alberta.

Dubnyk lost so much confidence in his final season with the Oilers that he was traded to the Nashville Predators. He started twice for the Predators, giving up nine goals in two games, before being dealt again, this time to the Montreal Canadiens.

He never appeared in a game for Montreal and instead was sent to their AHL affiliate. His wife, Jenn, had given birth to the couple's first son a few months prior, so Dubnyk asked if he could go home, a request that was granted.

Some believed his NHL career might be over. "I wasn't dumb. I mean, if I truly thought I would have had an opportunity, I wouldn't have gone anywhere," Dubnyk told TSN in 2016. "But it had been such an insane season, and I had a 10-month-old son at home. I hadn't seen him for 10 weeks. There's more important things I need to be doing in my life right now, and that's being a dad. The Canadiens were awesome about it. I just told them I had to go see my son and my wife."

The following summer, he ended up agreeing to a one-year, $800,000 contract as Mike Smith's backup with the Coyotes, a move that ended up changing his career. Arizona goalie coach Sean Burke helped get Dubnyk back on track, the goaltender regained his confidence, and by midseason the Coyotes bargain-bin find was about to net the club a third-round pick.

The deal ended up being one of the most lopsided trades in recent NHL history, a fact nobody could have predicted at the time.

Dubnyk took a red-eye flight from Phoenix to Buffalo, New York, to meet the Wild there, jamming his 6'6" frame into a middle seat in coach. The next night, he stopped all 18 shots he faced in a 7–0 Wild win against the Sabres.

With that, Minnesota had stumbled upon something special. The Wild went 10–1–2 in his first 13 starts, and Dubnyk started 39 of the Wild's 40 remaining games that season, posting a remarkable 27–9–2 record over that stretch, with a 1.78 goals-against average and a .936 save percentage, propelling the Wild back to the playoffs in the process. "You have to go through these things in life and in your career," Dubnyk said. "There's no way to know what it is you have to go through. Not everyone has to get traded or go down to the minors like I did. My journey is that I had to really crash and burn, and it took me to Arizona, where I was just so grateful at that point just to have a job in the NHL."

Minnesota re-signed Dubnyk to a lucrative contract extension a few months later, handing over a six-year, $26 million contract to a guy who one year prior signed for near the league minimum.

Those that questioned the wisdom of that contract extension were quickly quieted once again, as Dubnyk has proven to be one of the NHL's great bargains.

Over the first three years of the contract, Dubnyk ranked among the top five in the entire NHL in wins, goals-against average, save percentage, and minutes played. During the summer of 2018, Dubnyk's $4.3 million salary cap hit dropped out of the top 20 highest paid goaltenders in the league. "[Minnesota] is such a great place to raise a family; we enjoy it so much there," Dubnyk said. "Life is great. Gosh, it was so close to being a whole lot different than that."

74 The Wild Anthem

When the Wild began playing games in 2000, it needed little else to engage with fans for the first decade the franchise was back on the ice. Even after the lockout in 2005, which wiped out an entire season and caused buildings around the league to take some time to get back to capacity, the Xcel Energy Center had a line, quite literally, out the door and around the block waiting for tickets to the games once players and owners reached a new collective bargaining agreement.

During its early years, the team had a number of quirks that few others around the league had, including a lighthouse in the upper corner of the rink that shined every time the goal horn went off. It's a feature that remains inside the arena to this day.

In one of the other corners was a house band called the Hip Checks that would play live music between periods to entertain the fans.

Another quirk was "The Wild Anthem," or as some people call it, "The State of Hockey Song." It was written and composed by a former public relations mogul in the Twin Cities, John Olson, and played at the very first regular-season game in franchise history.

It's been played at every game since during the first intermission right before the Wild returns to the ice for the second period. Over the years, the video montage that accompanies it has changed with the times. "The words capture the craziness of the passion we have in this state for hockey," Wild president Matt Majka told a local television station in 2016. "It's a little quirky and a little campy."

"Campy" might be the perfect way to describe it. It sounds like a song you might sing around a bonfire during a week at summer camp in northern Minnesota.

For more than 15 years, the original version stood alone, until 2017, when a number of local bands took it and changed it into their own brand of music. Rock musicians, rappers, and country music singers, among others, took the original words, changed the score around, and created their own versions, selling their work to raise money for the Minnesota Wild Foundation.

But it's the original that stands out to regulars at Xcel Energy Center, an earworm of a song that can usually be learned word-for-word after just a couple of listens. Here is how it starts for the first three stanzas:

We were raised
with the stick
and a pair of blades.
On the ice we cut our teeth.
We took our knocks
in the penalty box.
Our mother was the referee.

This sport was here
before we came.
It will be here when we're gone.
The game's in our blood,
and our blood's in the game.
Lay us down under
a frozen pond.

We will fight to the end.
We will stand and defend
our flag flying high and free.
We were born the child
of the strong and Wild
in the state, the State of Hockey.

75 Fenton's Big Chance

It took nearly 20 years for Paul Fenton to finally get his chance as an NHL general manager, but in 2018, he got it with the Wild.

Fenton's playing career in the NHL was nothing special. He scored 100 goals in 411 games with seven different teams in eight seasons, once skating for the Toronto Maple Leafs, Winnipeg Jets, and Calgary Flames all in the span of one 82-game campaign (1990–91).

But where the Cambridge, Massachusetts, native has made his mark is in the player personnel world, helping to build two teams virtually from scratch. After retiring as a player following the 1991–92 season, Fenton was a scout with the then Mighty Ducks of Anaheim by 1993. He was part of a front office that drafted Paul Kariya that year, then traded for Teemu Selanne early in 1996.

After five years with the Ducks, Fenton went to Nashville to help build that team from the ground up. He started as the director of player personnel, a job he held for eight seasons before he was named the team's assistant general manager in the summer of 2006.

As the man in charge of Nashville's draft table, he played central roles in the drafting of guys like Ryan Suter, Shea Weber, and Pekka Rinne, among others. Along with general manager David Poile, Fenton was in the room as Nashville built a core that made a trip to the Stanley Cup Finals in 2017, acquiring players like James Neal, P.K. Subban, and Ryan Johansen through trades, and drafting others like Viktor Arvidsson, Roman Josi, Ryan Ellis, and Mattias Ekholm, among many, many others.

Despite all that success, Fenton had never been able to break away and nab his own operation until May 21, 2018, when Wild owner Craig Leipold and president Matt Majka tabbed Fenton to be the third GM in franchise history.

Wild owner Craig Leipold, left, poses with general manager Paul Fenton during Fenton's introductory press conference on May 22, 2018.

A month earlier, Leipold cut ties with previous general manager Chuck Fletcher, who had run the Wild for nine seasons and helped the team to playoff appearances in six consecutive years. But having only gotten past the first round twice during that span and never past the second round, Leipold wanted a change.

In Fenton he found someone he was familiar with and someone he had hired in Nashville when he owned the Predators two decades earlier. "I would say probably Paul was No. 1 on my list, and as we had our list and the list kept growing and we kept interviewing people, he just stayed No. 1. There were just so many what we felt were really important factors and qualities that we were looking for that Paul has," Leipold said. "After the second round of interviews, it was just clear that Paul was our guy."

Fenton, the son of a police chief, has a well-earned reputation as one of the hardest working men in all of professional hockey. As someone who has specialized in identifying young talent and then helping to develop it—a track record brandished in Nashville—Fenton has built relationships all over the world that have helped him pick talent from all areas of the draft. "It comes natural for me to look at a player and say, 'I like what he does,' or, 'I don't like what he does,'" Fenton said. "I can still put myself in their skates and kind of play out what they do."

One of Fenton's favorite stories to tell about how he got his work ethic comes from his days as a teenager when he played junior hockey in New England. During one game he got into a fight. His dad, Paul Fenton Sr., was in the crowd and disgusted by the antics, went back to the dressing room to find his son and let him know of his disapproval.

After the game, Fenton Sr. ran into the team's assistant general manager, Jack Ferreira, a man who would one day run several NHL franchises and serve as Fenton Jr.'s mentor in hockey. Ferreira looked at his father and said, "Chief, don't ever take the fire away from him."

Fenton wells up when he tells the story, a reminder of his father, who passed away in 2007. But it's a reminder of the blue-collar work ethic implanted in him by his parents, one that he carries with him to this day. "I'll bring fire here; I'll bring fire everywhere," Fenton said.

Though known for his work ethic, Fenton was ultimately deemed a poor fit and dismissed after just one season on the job, and the Wild hired Bill Guerin of the Pittsburgh Penguins to replace him.

76 Minnesota Fighting Saints

Most die-hard hockey fans of a certain age have heard stories of the Minnesota Fighting Saints, but not as many know the Fighting Saints were actually two different teams that played around the same time.

The original Fighting Saints began play in 1972 as one of the World Hockey Association's original 12 teams. It took a different approach to stocking its team, rostering Minnesotans by the bunches. According to the website Vintagemnhockey.com, the 1972–73 Fighting Saints had 11 players who were either native Minnesotans or American. This was at a time when a majority of teams didn't have a single American-born player on their roster. "We did that by design," Fighting Saints general manager Glen Sonmor said in an interview with *Minnesota Hockey Magazine* in 2013. "The North Stars were struggling at the time, and so we went and got some guys that were fun to watch."

Among the Minnesotans on the original roster were Mike Antonovich from Calumet, Keith Christensen from International Falls, and Dick Paradise from St. Paul.

Antonovich, listed at 5'6" and 155 pounds, played for Sonmor at the University of Minnesota. Despite his diminutive stature, Antonovich was one of those "fun" players that Sonmor was always on the lookout for.

The fact that he knew him from his days with the Gophers and that he was also from Minnesota was just a bonus. "Maybe he saw himself in me," Antonovich told the *St. Paul Pioneer Press* one week after Sonmor's passing in 2015. "We were both a little bit crazy. We both enjoyed people. We shared a lot of things in common. He took me under his wing, and I think he wanted me to be successful. It was, 'Here's a little guy, and nobody's giving him much of a chance. And I'm going to give this guy a chance.'"

The first incarnation of the Fighting Saints ceased operations midway through the 1975–76 season, rostering future Wild coach Bruce Boudreau, who was playing his first season of pro hockey.

Reshuffling in the NHL would bring the Fighting Saints back a year later, when the California Golden Seals moved to Cleveland to become the Barons. The WHA's Cleveland Crusaders relocated to St. Paul and became the Fighting Saints.

Despite a winning record midway through their first season back in the Twin Cities, the Fighting Saints were again folded when owner Nick Mileti was unable to find new local ownership of the club.

It was an unfortunate turn of events for players like Antonovich, who played for the Fighting Saints in each of the club's first four years before playing 12 games for the North Stars in 1975–76.

When the Fighting Saints returned in 1976, so did Antonovich, who was having perhaps his best season as a pro when the team folded for the final time. Through 42 games that season, Antonovich had 27 goals and 48 points. "Glen gave me the opportunity to be successful. He had a lot of faith in me—he told me that," Antonovich said. "He was the kind of guy who made everybody feel good. It wasn't just the stars or best players—it was everybody. It was like a family. We were a band of brothers because of him. It was like he was our dad, and he tried to treat us all the same. For me, it was kind of a fairy tale."

77 Watch a Game in Grand Forks

For certain, there are better places to hang out during a weekend in the wintertime than Grand Forks, North Dakota. No offense to the fine people in the Peace Garden State, but as cold as Minnesota is during the dark winter months, North Dakota might be one of the few states in the country that can make an honest-to-goodness case that it's colder.

That's especially true in Grand Forks. Located about as far east in North Dakota as can be, the town sits on the western banks of the Red River of the North, just across from East Grand Forks, Minnesota. To the west of the city is about 500 miles of rolling prairie with nothing but wind whipping across.

Still, you won't hear many folks in this part of the country complaining during the winter months because that means its hockey season, and for fans in Grand Forks, that's something.

Not unlike the frenzied state of Green Bay Packers fans to the east of Minnesota, University of North Dakota hockey fans live and die with their now "Fighting Hawks." And for a place that is as desolate and quiet as Grand Forks, its hockey hub might be the best collegiate arena in the country.

Ralph Engelstad Arena, which opened in October of 2001, is a building much like Xcel Energy Center in that it only seems to get better with age. That's because of the care and expense that went into building the arena in the first place.

Granite and marble floors are nearly everywhere. All seats are leather and adorned with cherrywood armrests. Its capacity reaches more than 11,000 on a nightly basis, but there isn't a bad seat in the house. "It's one of the most beautiful buildings we have in North America," NHL legend Wayne Gretzky told the *Fargo Forum* during a trip to the arena in 2005. "It's everything people have said about it."

And the team is pretty good. The University of North Dakota has won eight NCAA national championships, most recently in 2016, and has been to the NCAA tournament 32 times (as of 2019).

UND plays in arguably the most competitive college hockey conference in the country, the National Collegiate Hockey Conference, a league that boasted the national champion in four consecutive years from 2016–19.

Because Grand Forks is small town in everything other than its hockey, there are plenty of places to grab an affordable meal and a cheap, cold beer. Third Street near the river is home to a number of local joints with delicious food, but it's a short drive or a taxi ride from Ralph Engelstad Arena.

Grand Forks is just two hours south of Winnipeg, an easy drive north on Interstate 29 to the Canadian border, and another hour on Manitoba Highway 75. There are worse ways to spend a winter weekend than watching hockey in these two cities, checking out a UND game in Grand Forks on Friday and a Jets game in Winnipeg on Saturday. Even if you're not a fan of either team, it should be two items on every hockey fan's bucket list.

78 Circle of Trust

Former Wild coach Jacques Lemaire is remembered in Minnesota for employing what some fans and experts called a neutral zone trap.

It's a term associated with boring, low-scoring hockey games, but it's also worked tremendously well, especially around the time the Wild entered the league in 2000. The New Jersey Devils—with Lemaire as head coach—won a Stanley Cup using a similar system just five years earlier.

For the early 2000s Wild, which had Marian Gaborik as its only true offensive sniper, playing strong defense was a necessity. But it's a system that requires complete buy-in from the team, statistical accolades be damned.

What made the Wild a successful expansion franchise—far more so than its cousins, the Columbus Blue Jackets—was that it was built mostly of players that bought into the system.

Wes Walz, once a 100-plus point scorer as a junior hockey player, thrived as a checking center. Antti Laaksonen scored points as a collegian at the University of Denver and in the minor leagues early in his career, but he was often stapled to Walz's breezers in a checking role.

Even scorers like Gaborik were expected to play a strong 200-foot game to the point where the winger and the coach butted heads.

Walz remembered one story early in his tenure with the team when Lemaire felt a couple of the guys on the club were getting a little too big for their britches. "One day he went up to the whiteboard and he drew a big circle. Inside of it, he wrote, 'TEAM,'" Walz said. "With his French accent, he kind of had a goofy way of saying things, but he would say, 'If there's a guy inside the circle, and starts to go outside the circle, you gotta grab him by the collar and come on back. We're a team.'"

The message was simple enough, and it was received loud and clear by veterans like Walz, Darby Hendrickson, Andrew Brunette, and Jim Dowd, who were in charge of policing the locker room.

That was the beauty of Lemaire, Walz said. Despite all his successes as a player in Montreal and as a coach in new Jersey, Lemaire was rarely in the Wild's dressing room. When he'd enter and provide a short message, he'd leave and allow the guys in the room to do the heavy lifting. "It was the simplest way that he would say it, and he'd never mention any names," Walz said. "But guys knew and we knew what he was talking about."

St. Paul

St. Paul was a much different city in the mid-1990s than it is in the late 2010s.

Senator Norm Coleman, who served two terms as mayor of the city during its early transformative years, credits the return of professional hockey and the Minnesota Wild as perhaps the biggest reason for the capital city's millennium resurgence. "There's no question that the Wild have had a transformative impact on the city," Coleman said. "Not only that, but all the concerts and the high school hockey."

Former Vikings kicker Ryan Longwell once made a joke that Applebee's was the finest restaurant in Green Bay, where he had played the first nine seasons of his NFL career, a comment that was not well received back in northeast Wisconsin.

But it was a similar comment on a different scale that may have changed the fortunes of pro hockey in the state of Minnesota.

In 1996 the Hartford Whalers were looking for a potential new home. Their owner, Peter Karmanos, met with Coleman and Minnesota governor Arne Carlson about bringing the team to a renovated St. Paul Civic Center.

The deal was close…or even done, some might say. Karmanos, Carlson, and Coleman agreed to a handshake deal—the Whalers were coming to St. Paul.

Karmanos eventually visited the city and had a good meeting with many of its business leaders. But the following day, Karmanos phoned Coleman and said he just couldn't go through with it. "He said, 'I don't know if this city can support a team,'" Coleman recalled. "He said, 'The cost of the room at your best hotel is less than I have to charge for tickets to a hockey game.' I don't know if you can support a team. And he was right. At that point in time, there wasn't a lot going on in St. Paul, and we probably had some pretty cheap rates."

Karmanos eventually moved his team to Raleigh, where it became the Carolina Hurricanes. While it was a stinging defeat for Coleman, Carlson, and the state, it only solidified Coleman's urgency to bring a professional sports franchise—specifically a hockey team—to the city to help spur a turnaround.

Having been turned down by now two relocating franchises (the first incarnation of the Winnipeg Jets nearly moved to Minnesota earlier in the year), the state—and specifically Coleman and St. Paul—turned their focus to an expansion team.

In 1997 Minnesota was awarded one of four new franchises with a brand-new Xcel Energy Center helping pave the way for a revitalization of the city, one that still exists today.

Without professional hockey? "It would be profoundly different," Coleman said. "It would have been a different place today without that much to the negative."

Just how different would it be?

Around the same time the Xcel Energy Center was being built, there was a referendum on the ballot to pass a half-cent sales tax in the city that would have allowed for the construction of a new baseball stadium on St. Paul's west side.

The measure failed, one that Coleman called the most stinging defeat of his political career (a career that includes a failed reelection to the U.S. Senate, one he lost by just 312 votes out of nearly 2.9 million cast).

Citizens in St. Paul were concerned about the city's debt load. Had the referendum come a couple years later, and folks could see the positive effect Xcel Energy Center had on transforming downtown, Coleman believes the referendum would have passed with ease. "Just think about if that Twins stadium would have been on the west side of St. Paul with more than a million people coming to [the city]," Coleman said. "Do you have any doubt in your mind how transformative that would have been? But it didn't happen, and the west side today is still kind of the sleepy west side."

While baseball wasn't destined to come to St. Paul, hockey has had a tremendous impact on the state's capital city.

80 Matt Johnson's Header

The most iconic moment in the Wild's franchise history would never have happened if not for a forgotten play late in regulation by a guy who probably shouldn't have even been on the ice in the first place.

And by forgotten, it's only by fans. The guys who were on the ice certainly haven't forgotten it at all.

With the underdog Wild knotted in a 2–2 tie with the Colorado Avalanche late in the third period of Game 7 at the Pepsi Center in Denver, coach Jacques Lemaire threw fourth-line brawler Matt Johnson over the boards.

Only this wasn't a typical time for Johnson to be on the ice. He took a total of nine shifts in the entire game, tallying just over three minutes of ice time.

But it was how his ninth shift ended that will endear him to his teammates forever. "I don't know why Matt was out there," said former Wild forward Wes Walz. "Maybe it was because we were all so gassed, and Jacques just felt that he needed to get that line out for one shift just to give the guys a blow."

With Colorado pushing, Avalanche defenseman Derek Morris gained control of a loose puck and moved toward the high slot. Johnson was caught out of position as the Colorado blue liner with a blistering shot wound up to fire from a prime scoring area.

Walz, sitting on the bench, had the perfect angle to see what happened next. "[Johnson] took inside ice and basically skated to the slot area, knowing he needed to try and find a way to block this," Walz said. "Then he dove. And if I wouldn't have seen it with my own eyes, I wouldn't have believed it. He dove in front of the slap shot with his head. And the puck hit his helmet and went up into the stands. I'll never forget it."

Walz said he remembered looking at the guy next to him on the bench and simply saying, "Wow." "We couldn't believe it," Walz said. "We couldn't believe what we just saw. He tried to block a slap shot with his head. That's how committed guys were to doing whatever it took to help the team."

Also on the bench, former Wild goaltender Dwayne Roloson remembered feeling the exact same thing. "It gave us the belief. We said, 'If Matt's doing that, let's follow his lead,'" Roloson said.

"We're all third or fourth line guys. Matt is going out there and sticking his head on the line. Derek Morris is no slouch when he's stepping into a slap shot or a one-timer, so for him to do that, I don't think anybody would want to do it. Matt knew it was going to hurt, but he just laid down and did it. That's what it was going to take to win the game."

Minnesota ended up getting the game to overtime before scoring the game-winning goal by Andrew Brunette 3:25 into the extra session.

The Wild would overcome a 3–1 series deficit in the next round against the Vancouver Canucks, advancing to the Western Conference Finals. To this date, the Wild are the only team in NHL history to overcome a pair of 3–1 series deficits in one playoff season.

To the guys in the uniform, Johnson's header was one of those turning-point moments during that run. "Our team was just like, 'Hey, Matt's out there doing whatever it takes to win,'" Roloson said. "Everyone started believing in themselves and doing a little bit extra."

81 Craig Leipold

Each preseason, Wild owner Craig Leipold invites a number of local media members into his suite to watch a game with him and between periods he chats with them and answers any questions about the upcoming season.

Leipold is a true social butterfly, and it's easy to see that the exercise is more than him simply placating local scribes and TV people; he genuinely enjoys meeting with the people that cover his team on a daily basis as long as the chatter is kept to a minimum while there is action on the ice.

Leipold sits in his center-ice suite at Xcel Energy Center intently watching the game with as much focus and attention as the general manager above him in the press box or the head coach behind the bench below him.

With a rolled up program in one hand, Leipold isn't afraid to whack the seat he's sitting on if there's a goal against or a development against the Wild. He's also the first on his feet clapping when the Wild scores a goal.

And never, ever try and sit next to him while the game is going on.

During the 2015 preseason, a local television reporter who was new to town learned this lesson the hard way. With Leipold intently watching the game, this reporter spotted an opportunity to hop down and thank the owner for his hospitality and to introduce himself.

It was, after all, a preseason game.

So down the stairs he went to the second row of seats where Leipold plops himself for every game. He sat down in the chair next to Leipold and extended his hand for an introduction.

All of a sudden, the suite filled with media members fell silent—amazed at this accidental breach of protocol. Leipold politely shook his hand, then looked to the people sitting and standing behind him in wonderment.

The reporter was briefed on Leipold's game-watching tradition—an empty seat next to him at all times—and quickly left for the back of the suite embarrassed, probably thinking he'd just made the biggest mistake of his young career. Leipold turned around and laughed. "Did you see the look on his face?" he howled.

Ever since he got into hockey ownership—first with the Nashville Predators, then with the Wild—Leipold has been one of his team's biggest fans. The original owner of the Predators, the

Racine, Wisconsin, native nearly became an NBA owner prior to venturing into hockey. He tried to buy both the Milwaukee Bucks and the Sacramento Kings but was unsuccessful.

It was then that he turned his attention to the NHL. "It was a time I was kind of kicking tires and checking what was available in the market. And at that time, I knew basketball better than I knew hockey," Leipold told *Sports Business Journal* in 2008. "As I wanted to get into sports business, I gravitated toward basketball. I didn't realize that those opportunities just weren't out there at the time and that hockey was. I'm just thrilled to death that, as it turned out, it was hockey."

Leipold was awarded the Nashville franchise in 1997, the same year the Wild were awarded to original team owner Bob Naegele. The Predators began play in 1998, and Leipold owned the team until December of 2007 before selling to a group of mostly local business owners who promised to keep in the team in Tennessee.

Within a month, Leipold regretted the move.

While the Predators were hemorrhaging money during his time as owner, Leipold had grown to love the game of hockey and missed it. With Naegele ready to sell the Wild, Leipold stepped in and purchased the club, finalizing the sale in April of 2008 just four months after relinquishing control of the Predators.

In buying the Wild, Leipold had walked into one of the NHL's most successful business models in one of its most passionate marketplaces. "This is a hockey market," Leipold said. "One of the great things this franchise has done is that it has really nurtured and protected the brand. In this market the Wild represents more than just hockey. It's a culture, a way of life."

82 Realignment

Prior to the 2013–14 season, the Wild were banished to the far northwest reaches of the National Hockey League. With no clout and little reason to complain, the NHL washed its hands of tricky division geography by placing the expansion Wild in the Northwest Division.

That meant a handful of games each season in Vancouver, Edmonton, Calgary, and Colorado—all four teams located at least one, and in the case of the Canucks, two time zones behind the Wild.

Start times of 9:10 PM local were the norm, with games finishing just shy of midnight. Not ideal television viewing for fans back home, especially during a workweek. At the same time, few cared. The NHL was back in Minnesota, and if that meant a schedule chock-full of games starting late at night, so be it.

But after more than a decade of these late nights and with new ownership in place following the sale of the team to Craig Leipold in 2008, the desire to reestablish rivalries the North Stars used to have grew. Soon, Leipold was leading the charge to get the Wild into a division with more traditional rivals like the Chicago Blackhawks and St. Louis Blues and, later, the Winnipeg Jets.

Finally, on March 14, 2013, Wild fans—and their owner—got their wish. The NHL approved realignment that moved the team away from its rivals in northwest Canada to ones located (mostly) in the Central time zone. Instead of late-night trips across the border, where customs often delayed arrivals until 3:00 or 4:00 AM in the Twin Cities, the Wild's longest intra-division flight became a two-hour excursion from Dallas. "It's a big deal for our franchise," former Wild general manager Chuck Fletcher told the *Minneapolis*

Star-Tribune. "It's a great opportunity for our team to reestablish some of the regional rivalries that the North Stars used to have a while back. It should be great. You can see the emotion in the building when Chicago and St. Louis and teams like that come into our building."

Along with realignment came divisional playoffs. No longer were teams seeded in the conference 1–8; instead, the top three teams in each division were guaranteed a postseason spot while two wild-cards were also granted entry. This format was modeled after the old Norris Division battles. The belief was that repeated encounters in the playoffs would spice up rivalries.

It didn't take long for realignment and the new playoff format to do just that for the Wild. Minnesota faced the Chicago Blackhawks in three consecutive playoffs, losing all three times to their rivals from the south.

The Wild also faced the Blues twice in the span of three years between 2015 and 2017.

During its stretch of six consecutive playoff berths from 2013–18, the Wild has faced every team in its division, save Nashville, in a playoff series, accomplishing exactly what the NHL hoped it would when it brought regional rivals back together again.

Darby

There's a reason why those that know and work with Darby Hendrickson on a daily basis call him "The Governor."

It's a nickname earned after a lifetime of hockey memories made in Minnesota, where the Richfield native starred at the high school and college levels before becoming one of the most beloved members of the earliest Wild teams.

Minnesota Wild center Darby Hendrickson sends the puck past Philadelphia Flyers goalie Brian Boucher for the first goal in Wild history.

Hendrickson was born August 28, 1972, in Richfield, into a hockey-centric family. His dad, the legendary Larry Hendrickson, played at Minneapolis Washburn, then coached Richfield and Apple Valley High Schools to the state tournament, winning a championship with the latter in 1996.

His younger brother, Danny, played hockey at Richfield and the University of Minnesota, just like Darby did. "For me college was a huge thing," Darby Hendrickson said in an interview with *The Hockey News*. "The NHL was a dream, but the other ones were more tangible, where you want to play for your high school hockey team."

It was Darby who would go the furthest in the game. A fourth-round pick of the Toronto Maple Leafs in the 1990 NHL Draft, Hendrickson made his NHL debut with the Leafs during the 1994–95 season, his first of five seasons with the Leafs.

Hendrickson was never able to find the same scoring touch he had growing up, however, scoring 11 goals in 64 games with Toronto in 1996–97. He couldn't find regular ice time either, reaching the 80-game mark just once in his first six seasons at the NHL level.

After a year and a half with the Vancouver Canucks, the team made him available for the expansion draft in 2000, where his hometown team pounced, making him one of their 26 selections that day.

For Hendrickson, the opportunity to come home was a personal one. Like many of his era who grew up watching the North Stars, he was stung when the team left for Dallas in 1993. "A lot of these guys were guys you wanted to be like when you were a kid, to somehow reach their level," Hendrickson said. "That void, when the North Stars left [in 1993], kids didn't have that anymore. When they left, everybody lost a little bit."

Only a handful of players picked by Minnesota at the expansion draft would go on to have any sort of meaningful impact with the Wild, but Hendrickson was certainly one of them. He scored the first goal in Xcel Energy Center history on October 11, 2000, against the Philadelphia Flyers.

Hendrickson played in 72 games with the Wild during its inaugural season and posted a career bests with 18 goals, 11 assists, and 29 points, while also posting an even digit in the plus/minus category.

He followed it up with another solid season the next year, scoring nine goals and 24 points in 68 games.

During the Wild's run to the Western Conference Finals in 2003, Hendrickson would prove valuable, scoring a pair of goals and dishing out three assists during Minnesota's 17-game post-season run. One of those goals was the game-winner in Game 7 against his former team, the Canucks, as the Wild bounced back from a 3–1 series deficit for the second time in as many series. To this date, the Wild are the only team in NHL history to come back from two 3–1 series deficits in a single playoff series.

Hendrickson played in just 14 games with the Wild in 2003–04 before moving on to the Colorado Avalanche, where he skated in 20 more games.

The NHL lockout that wiped out the entire 2004–05 season effectively ended Hendrickson's playing career. He played two more seasons in Austria before calling it quits as a player and returning to Minnesota, where he began a career as a broadcaster.

In 2011 Hendrickson was brought on the Wild's coaching staff by first-year coach Mike Yeo. His value as the staff's "eye in the sky" has been immeasurable, as Hendrickson has kept his position through three different head coaches.

His playing career with the Wild during their first two years and his contributions during the team's long playoff run in year three endeared him to the Wild's first generation of fans. To them, he's not just a player or a coach. He's "The Governor."

84 Getting Its Guy

The Wild selected Mikko Koivu with the sixth pick in the 2001 NHL Draft, but it's interesting to think about the road not travelled. It was no secret that the Montreal Canadiens, picking one slot behind the Wild that summer, were interested in Koivu; his older brother, Saku, was named the 27th captain in Canadiens history some two years prior, and the opportunity to unite the brothers on the same team had executives salivating.

Sitting at the Wild's draft table, however, were general manager Doug Risebrough, head coach Jacques Lemaire, and scout Guy Lapointe, each of which had legendary playing careers in Montreal.

The Wild, like the Canadiens, loved the idea of adding Koivu, a big, two-way centerman, to its fold. But according to Tom Lynn, the club's first assistant general manager, Minnesota had some roadblocks to navigate.

First, it picked sixth, and unless it was willing to sacrifice assets to move up, Minnesota would have to hope the five teams in front of it would pass on Koivu. Second, it had to hope the Canadiens—or any other team picking behind them—didn't sense Minnesota's interest and jump in front of the Wild with a trade of its own. "Doug even went so far as to discuss at length how important goaltending was to the long-term success of the franchise," Lynn wrote in his book, *How to Bake an NHL Franchise From Scratch: The First Era of the Minnesota Wild.* "Only a few of us knew the real plan."

Koivu finished the scouting season ranked fourth among European skaters according to NHL Central Scouting, and Ilya Kovalchuk and Jason Spezza were heavy favorites to be picked 1–2 in the draft.

Everything went as planned early. The Atlanta Thrashers took Kovalchuk with the first pick, and the Ottawa Senators nabbed Spezza second. Alexander Svitov, ranked second among Euro skaters after Kovalchuk, was picked third by Tampa Bay. Florida went with centerman Stephen Weiss fourth overall, putting the Mighty Ducks of Anaheim on the clock. "The team we always felt was most likely to take Koivu was Anaheim," Lynn wrote in his book. "I stared straight at my computer screen, trying not to move a muscle."

Koivu, top-rated defenseman Mike Komisarek, and skilled—but diminutive—Russian forward Stanislav Chistov were among the Ducks' most likely selections. "As the Florida group made its way down to the podium, Anaheim GM Pierre Gauthier smiled and turned to Doug and said, 'It's going to be the little guy,'" Lynn wrote.

Thrilled with the turn of events, the Wild gladly selected Koivu with the sixth pick, much to the chagrin of the Canadiens. "Fists slammed the table, French curse words were mumbled, and glares were exchanged," Lynn wrote. "The Wild's ruse had worked, and the Montreal staff was none too happy about it."

Koivu has been arguably the best player in franchise history for the Wild, becoming the club's first permanent captain in 2009 and ranking as the franchise's leader in nearly every offensive category.

Al Shaver

For many fans in the State of Hockey, the voice narrating the sport will always be longtime North Stars broadcaster Al Shaver. How many fell asleep at night to the dulcet tones of Shaver reverberating through their pillows, a radio stuffed secretly away?

For 26 years Shaver was the man behind the microphone at Met Center. A Canadian by birth, Shaver began his legendary career north of the border, graduating from the Lorne Greene Academy of Radio and Television Arts in Toronto in 1948. From there, he went up and down the radio dial with stops in Guelph, Ontario, before heading west to Calgary, Medicine Hat, and Edmonton, where he called Eskimos games for the Canadian Football League club.

Stops in Montreal and Toronto preceded his trek south to Minnesota, where he was named the North Stars radio voice upon the team's entry into the NHL in 1967. For 11 years Shaver called games on a legendary frequency, AM 830 WCCO out of Minneapolis. On a clear night, the station could be heard across the state and all around the Upper Midwest. Some even said they've heard the station clearly as far away as California.

In 1978 the North Stars and Shaver moved to AM 1500 KSTP until they moved to Dallas following the 1992–93 season. By the time the team left, Shaver had become royalty in Minnesota, and when the club went south, he stayed behind, calling University of Minnesota hockey games for three seasons until hanging up his headset in 1996.

His call of the final moments of the last North Stars game in 1993 is one that remains in the minds of fans across Minnesota, a sad reminder that the state's hockey team was not only wrapping up its season, but also packing its bags: "The Stars lose it here 5–3, and now it's pack-'em-up time and on to Dallas. We wish them good luck. And to all the North Stars over the past 26 years, we say thank you, all of you, for so much fine entertainment.

"It's been a pleasure knowing you, Minnesota's loss is definitely a gain for Dallas—and a big one. We thank you, though, from the bottoms of our hearts, for all the wonderful nights at Met Center, when you've given us so much entertainment, and you've been such a credit to the community in which you played. "We will still remember you as the Minnesota North Stars. Good night, everybody. And good-bye."

Al Shaver's legacy remains strong in Minnesota. His son, Wally Shaver, has been calling Gophers men's hockey games for two decades. Al Shaver left retirement in 2000, calling Wild games during the team's inaugural season. The press box inside Xcel Energy Center was named the "Al Shaver Press Box" in his honor.

After retirement Shaver and his wife, Shirley, moved back to Canada, settling in the Vancouver area. A 10-time winner of Minnesota's Broadcaster of the Year award, Shaver is a member of both the Minnesota Broadcasting Hall of Fame and the Hockey Hall of Fame in Toronto.

86 The Burns Trade

When the Wild drafted Brent Burns with the 20th pick in the 2003 NHL Entry Draft, it wasn't quite sure what it had in the Ajax, Ontario, native. Burns came up as a right wing but was never a big-time scorer at the junior level. His best offensive season came the season before he was drafted when he scored 15 goals and 40 points in 68 games with the Brampton Battalion.

Burns played in 36 games with the Wild in 2003–04 as coach Jacques Lemaire got his hands on the physical imposing forward. At 6'5" and well over 200 pounds, perhaps Burns' best attribute was his ability to move at that size.

Lemaire, seemingly always thinking about defense, decided to try converting Burns to defenseman. Despite some wavering early— Burns moved back and forth between the positions early on—the move worked out brilliantly. "Pregame skates as a d-man, warm up as a winger, game maybe both," Burns told NBC California in 2016, the year he was a finalist for the Norris Trophy. "At that time I was young; it kind of took a lot of stress off. It was fun. I learned a lot from [Lemaire], too." Unfortunately for the Wild, much of the fruit of that labor came with Burns in a different uniform.

Following the lockout season in 2004–05, Burns was locked in on the Wild blue line, scoring four goals and 16 points in 72 games. Those numbers only got better each of the next two seasons. By 2007–08, Burns played in 82 games and scored 15 goals. His last season with Minnesota, Burns skated in 80 games and had 17 goals and 46 points.

A pending unrestricted free agent in 2012 and still just 26 years old, Burns was about to get paid. It was a number Wild general manager Chuck Fletcher, who had taken over for Doug Risebrough two years prior, was unsure he was willing to meet.

So on June 24, 2011, as the first round of the NHL Draft was taking place (at Xcel Energy Center), the Wild sent Burns and a second-round pick to the San Jose Sharks in exchange for forward Devin Setoguchi, prospect Charlie Coyle, and a first-round pick (28th overall). "It was very difficult," Fletcher said of the decision. "I just look at our team right now, and we really need to aggressively add young players. The last two years have been disappointing. We've obviously talked about that. But in order to compete with the top teams in this league, we have to have more talent."

Fans inside the arena were none too pleased. Burns was a fan favorite, and his quirkiness had developed a bit of a cult following in the Twin Cities. He was a fan of animals, and his suburban Twin Cities home had earned the nickname "Burns Zoo" because of the multitude of different creatures on his property.

Burns career took off in San Jose. He was moved to back to forward early in his time with the Sharks, but he has played mostly defense since the 2014–15 campaign. Burns posted five consecutive 60-plus point seasons from the back end, including two 27-plus goal, 75-plus point campaigns in the 2015–16 and 2016–17 seasons, which earned him another long-term contract from the Sharks.

The Wild, meanwhile, never got what it hoped for out of Setoguchi, a three-time, 20-plus goal scorer with the Sharks who posted 31 goals in his second season in the NHL in 2008–09 as a 22-year-old. Setoguchi scored a total of 32 goals in 117 games over two seasons with the Wild but wasn't the right fit in the dressing

room. Minnesota traded him to Winnipeg during the summer of
2013, and he was out of the NHL by the time he was 30.

Coyle was the best player to come out of the trade for the Wild,
as the rangy forward played in more than 400 games with the club
until he was traded to his hometown Boston Bruins in February of
2019 for young forward Ryan Donato.

With their first-round pick, the Wild selected forward Zack
Phillips of the Quebec Major Junior Hockey League. The selection
was disastrous, as Phillips never came close to reaching the NHL.
Among players selected within 30 picks of Phillips in the draft that
season were Rickard Rakell (30th), John Gibson (39th), Brandon
Saad (43rd), and perhaps the most painful of all, Nikita Kucherov
(58th). Picking any of those four likely would have made the trade
far more palatable for Wild fans.

87 Matt Majka

The raw emotion on Matt Majka's face is real anytime he talks
about the signings of Zach Parise and Ryan Suter. One of the few
employees remaining with the organization from its earliest days
pre-2000, Majka has been a part of it all. He came to the Wild
with original owner Bob Naegele, who brought him with from
Rollerblade, the company he owned for a decade back in the 1980s
and '90s.

Majka had never worked in hockey, but after spending 14 years
at Rollerblade, he was ready for something different and he believed
the Wild had a chance to be something special. Majka came aboard
at a unique time in the organization's timeline, when it had no
players or coaches, no arena to call home, no logo or colors or

history to speak of. When Majka started, the team was known only as "Minnesota NHL."

"There were a lot of marketing initiatives that grew out of those early days, and of course, the team name was a big part of it," Majka said. He brought his marketing savvy to the table and has been a part of nearly every major decision in the franchise's history, from asking teams to submit their choices for a name, to picking a name and colors, to designing and marketing Xcel Energy Center all the way to present day, where he serves as the president and alternate governor.

During his time the team has announced numerous initiatives supporting youth and women's hockey in the state, as well as wide-ranging marketing ideas like the "State of Hockey" concept and the current "This Is Our Ice" theme, both of which have been tremendously popular with fans.

Few people inside the organization have the tangible connection to it that Majka has, from the look and design of the uniforms to its marketing initiatives to his work in 2018 with owner Craig Leipold to help land Paul Fenton as the team's third general manager.

There is literally no area of the team that Majka hasn't had a hand in helping to build since he joined the club in 1997. That's why he still gets emotional about Suter and Parise, perhaps the biggest landmark day in the franchise's history, save for the day it was awarded a team.

In July of 2012, the team had played 11 seasons, but there was no doubt the appeal of having NHL hockey back in Minnesota was starting to wear off with local fans. The Wild's shutout streak, which had lasted more than 10 years, had ended a couple years prior, and their season-ticket base was shrinking. "Absolutely, no question about it," Majka said. "[The honeymoon] finally had [ended], it took a lot longer than I thought it would and anyone could have expected, but it had. It clearly had. We were gravely concerned about it."

The Wild had made the postseason three times in team history but had advanced past the first round just once. At that point in time, it had been nearly a decade since the Wild's magical run to the Western Conference Finals in 2003.

Fans were no longer interested in just having a team…they wanted a winning team. And it was clear something major needed to be done. "We were in a bad spot," Majka said. "We had struggled to make the playoffs for four or five straight years, and our roster needed serious help. The vibe around the team was low, and the season-ticket base was shrinking."

Chuck Fletcher, the team's general manager at the time, had an ambitious idea: sign Suter or Parise, a plan that eventually morphed into signing both players. It was a longshot, but it was the shot in the arm the organization needed.

On July 4, 2012, the team's fax machine buzzed, and across the wire came signed deals from both players.

Immediately, the Wild's fortunes turned. "Everybody in the office walked a little taller after that," Majka said. "I give Chuck and Craig a ton of credit; Chuck put together a plan to go get those two. We went down to our annual planning retreat in May, and Chuck brought his plan along to get those two, and he said, 'Craig, I think we need to try. If we're lucky, we might get one. But here's the plan on how we're going to do it.' Craig looked at it, he looked at the season-ticket numbers and what was happening, and he said, 'Let's go, let's get one of them.'"

Overnight, season-ticket sales were booming. The team's waiting list for tickets, cleverly named the "Warming House," was filling back up. The direction of the team changed, as evidenced by its six consecutive playoff berths in the years after the signing, and it was now on solid footing for the first time since its earliest years.

For folks like Majka, who had been there from the beginning, it was like an organizational rebirth. "It was transformative and unifying for the organization," Majka said. "We were optimistic. We got our groove back again. If neither one of them had come, I shudder to think about how the business would have looked that following year. And who knows, maybe the team would have found its identity a different way, but I don't even want to think about it. It really just was a pivot point for the organization."

88 John Mayasich

One of the true legends of Minnesota hockey, John Mayasich never played in the National Hockey League following a standout career at Eveleth High School and the University of Minnesota. Many believe the only reason Mayasich doesn't get his credit as one of the sport's all-time greats is the era in which he played in. "Like a lot of great American players of his era, John came along at the wrong time," the legendary Herb Brooks said in an interview with *Sports Illustrated*. "He had a great shot and was a tremendous playmaker and skater, but what set him apart was that he was the smartest hockey player I've been around. He was subtle, like a great chess master, and he made players around him better. It was like he saw the game in slow motion."

Because Mayasich grew up at a time before television, he spent nearly every waking hour playing sports. He was a natural in baseball and football, too, but it was hockey where he gained what limited fame he has. "We didn't have hockey nets. We just used a pair of boots as the goal. If you shot the puck, you'd have to spend the next 10 minutes looking for it in the snowbank," Mayasich told *SI*. "So we always deked the goalies, and I became a pretty good stickhandler. I learned to shoot backhand from playing street hockey, where the goals weren't opposite one another because we didn't have enough room. You were always coming at them from an angle."

Between 1948 and 1951, Mayasich led the Eveleth Golden Bears to four consecutive state high school championships, winning 69 games during that stretch and losing none. No team before or since has accomplished that feat, and those Eveleth teams are considered some of the greatest in state history.

After that he went to the University of Minnesota on a football scholarship but never suited up for the team. Instead, he played hockey, where he would carve out a career paralleled by none in the history of the program.

While with the Gophers, Mayasich mastered the slap shot, something that was rarely used at the time, and when it was, it was at much higher levels.

Mayasich credited his old teammate at Eveleth, Willard Ikola, a goaltender on the state championship clubs that went to the University of Michigan. Ikola's Wolverines scrimmaged the Detroit Red Wings each year, and it was there where Ikola first saw the shot.

Back in Eveleth for the summer, Ikola described the shot to Mayasich, who had never seen it. What made the shot more difficult was that players didn't use curved sticks at the time. "I worked on it quite a bit," Mayasich said. "I had strong wrists from baseball and tennis and got to where I could really let it go. If I was aiming at the right pipe, I'd come within six inches most of the time. I'd use it when I came down three-on-two, waiting till the defense backed in enough to let me get across the blue line. Then I'd slap it, and if the goalie stopped it, there was usually a rebound. If the defense held the blue line, I'd pass off to a wing."

Mayasich's 144 goals and 298 points in just 111 games at the University of Minnesota still stand as university records, and his No. 8 jersey is the only one in school history to be retired.

But somehow, Mayasich was never given a chance to play in the NHL. College players were considered long shots to reach the league at the time, and with only six teams—all with Canadian-born general managers—few in college ever got a shot. "It wasn't a source of bitterness since no college players were being given a chance," Mayasich said. "But there's still regret, even to this day, not knowing if I could have done it."

Mayasich won a silver medal with the United States at the 1956 Olympics. By 1960 Mayasich was working in television advertising and was playing with a top amateur team in Green Bay, Wisconsin. He didn't join the 1960 Olympic team until shortly before the Games, practicing once with the team before posting a hat trick in the opening contest of the Games. He led the team to a surprising gold medal in 1960 in Squaw Valley, an achievement known as "The Forgotten Miracle."

Despite that his standout performance opened no doors for him at the professional level. "There's no doubt he could have played in the NHL," Jack McCartan told *SI*. McCartan was the goalie for the U.S. in 1960 and reached the NHL with the New York Rangers. "He was the best American hockey player I've ever seen."

89 Elephant Dung

Former United States senator and two-term mayor of St. Paul, Norm Coleman is one of the main forces behind bringing hockey back to Minnesota in 1997. Professional hockey in Minnesota likely wouldn't exist in Minnesota without his dogged determination. At the very least, the landscape would look completely different.

One of Coleman's favorite stories about the return of hockey came shortly before the league announced it was making its return into the Minnesota marketplace. Coleman and a number of other business and civic leaders were showing NHL commissioner Gary Bettman around town. That included a stop at the St. Paul Civic Center, which at the time was going to be renovated to help woo a team to the city.

As the group toured the more than two-decade-old facility, there was a strong odor emanating from the legendary building. "The day before the tour, the circus was in town, and they had just moved out," Coleman said. "And if you know the Civic Center, it was kind of 1950s East German architecture, a round cement building with no windows. Our plan was to renovate it, but the smell of elephant dung was hot and heavy. We were walking through this place, and it looked bad and smelled bad."

Coleman, along with Jac Sperling, believed the city had an ownership group headed by Bob Naegele that was first class. They knew Minnesota was a passionate hockey market with hundreds of thousands of passionate fans, many of whom still played the sport, even at advanced ages.

But while the St. Paul Civic Center certainly had its charms about it, on this particular day, it was not helping the group's cause. "I don't know if [Jac] graded it a D or an F," Coleman recalled. "But he had to grade it like that, or otherwise all of our credibility would have been gone. He was honest about it."

It all ended up working out, however. "I remember Bettman leaning over to me and whispering, 'You guys are gonna have to get a new facility,'" Coleman said. "And I knew it. Jac knew it. So we left that meeting and we had to come up with another plan to build a new arena and figure out how to build a new facility. That was not the plan originally."

Bettman left town that day, but the sour first impression didn't spoil things. Coleman, Sperling, and their teams worked together to craft a plan for a new arena that would become Xcel Energy Center. Not long after, Bettman returned with good news: the NHL was coming back to Minnesota.

90 Hit the Ice at the Wells Fargo WinterSkate

While there are tens of thousands of outdoor skating rinks in Minnesota, how many are in the heart of downtown St. Paul, steps from Xcel Energy Center, nestled among the skyscrapers?

Located next door to the famous Landmark Center in downtown, the Wells Fargo WinterSkate provides a picturesque backdrop for anyone looking to lace up the skates and hit the ice in just a setting.

The best part about the WinterSkate is that it never closes when it's too warm out. Because its ice sheet is refrigerated, the only time the park closes is when it's too cold to be outside—minus-25 degrees air temperature or wind chill.

The rink is also closed on Christmas Day and New Year's Day, but it's open virtually every other day during Minnesota's long winter months, beginning in early December and lasting until mid-February.

In addition to family skating, the WinterSkate also plays host to youth hockey games and practices as well as corporate broomball events.

During the week, the rink opens each day for public use at 11:00 AM Monday through Thursday, it's open until 4:50 PM before it is cleared for scheduled events. On Fridays and Saturdays, it's open until 10:00 PM and is used by the public all day long. On Sundays, it's open until 4:50 PM.

It's also a cheap place to bring the family. It's free to use the WinterSkate, though skaters under the age of 18 must sign a waiver. Don't have skates? You can rent them from the park for just $4 per person (Wells Fargo customers get one free rental by showing their debit or credit card.) Free skating lessons are also available in December and January.

91 Natalie Darwitz

When Natalie Darwitz first became a household name in Minnesota hockey circles, she was in seventh grade playing up with the Eagan High School varsity team. She was so good during her high school years that, despite starting her varsity career as a seventh grader, she still played just four years of high school hockey. By the time she was a junior, Darwitz was so advanced she had moved on to the U.S. national team.

The Darwitz effect can be seen in Eagan's success at that time. The girls' hockey program began at EHS in 1996, when the Wildcats went 11–11–0 in 22 games. Over the next four years, all with Darwitz in the fold, Eagan lost a total of 13 games, posting a 92–13–2 record. They won three conference championships and three sectional championships and played in three state tournaments, finishing as the runner-up in 1997, Darwitz's first season.

In all four of her seasons, Darwitz finished as an All-State selection, winning the Associated Press State Player of the Year in 1999, when she was just a freshman. Three times, Darwitz finished on the All-Tournament team at the state tournament.

In 102 games as a high school player, Darwitz compiled a ridiculous 487 points, an average of 4.77 points per game.

She was the first girls' hockey superstar in state history. "I just saw the ice really well and was more of playmaker," Darwitz told *Minnesota Hockey* in 2016. "I probably was a little bit of a combination of the hockey IQ and awareness of Zach Parise but with the quickness and explosiveness of Jason Zucker."

That hockey IQ likely came from her dad, Scott, who coached her in high school. After a standout career with the University of Minnesota, where she was a three-time All-American and won two national championships, and a brilliant career on the international stage, where she played in three Olympic games, eight world championships, and 10 Four Nations Cups, Darwitz first got into coaching as an assistant with her dad back at Eagan High School.

With the Golden Gophers, Darwitz continued her prodigious scoring totals, posting 246 points (third-most in program history) and averaging 2.48 points per game, a number that ranks first in school history. Her 144 assists are third.

The 2005 Women's Hockey Player of the Year as awarded by USA Hockey, Darwitz quickly rose up the coaching ladder, going from Eagan to the University of Minnesota as an assistant before going back to the high school ranks and taking over Lakeville South High School. In four years there, she went 79–25–10 and brought the team to its first state tournament.

In 2015 Darwitz moved to the Division III ranks, becoming head coach of Hamline University's women's team. The club improved by three wins between her first and second years with the Pipers and by 10 more wins from year two to year three, proving that Darwitz is a winner in virtually everything she does.

A true pioneer in girls' and women's hockey, she became the first female to practice with the Minnesota Wild in December of 2016, helping to kick off girls' hockey weekend in the state. One of her teammates—at least for a day—was Wild forward Parise, who actually played on her team when the two were kids growing up in the southern Twin Cities metro. Parise was from next-door Bloomington. "She was always our best player," Parise said. "It was neat to fast-forward all these years and see her on the ice again and watch her out there."

In 2018 she was inducted into the United States Hockey Hall of Fame in Eveleth, becoming the first Minnesota-born woman to be inducted.

92 Jac Sperling

How in the world did a guy born and raised in New Orleans end up being one of the major players for the Wild during its formative years in Minnesota? You can thank former St. Paul mayor and senator Norm Coleman for that.

Back in the mid-1990s, Sperling was working with then Winnipeg Jets owner Richard Burke on a relocation plan. The Twin Cities, without a team for two years following the North Stars' departure to Dallas, was a potential landing spot.

Set on making St. Paul a major player, Coleman was doing everything he could to bring the Jets to the city.

The only problem was, the St. Paul Civic Center was not a truly viable facility to host an NHL team, and Xcel Energy Center was not on the minds of anyone just yet.

Burke's group focused on Minneapolis, an opportunity that eventually fell through, and later on Phoenix, Arizona, where the Jets would later move to and become the Coyotes.

"The timing wasn't quite right," Sperling said of St. Paul's desire to lure the Jets. But Coleman's dream of bringing pro sports to St. Paul didn't die there. He asked Burke for advice on how he could best bring the NHL to the city. "You should hire Jac," Burke said, according to Sperling.

Coleman did just that, bringing Sperling aboard with the Capital City Partnership, a group intent on bringing a pro hockey team to Minnesota's capital city. "He was an absolute ace," Coleman said. "One of the best things I ever did was hire him."

Two years after joining the Capital City Partnership, the city of St. Paul was awarded an expansion franchise, joining the NHL along with the Columbus Blue Jackets as the league's 29th and 30th franchises. "It was not a straight line, and there were some challenges," Sperling said. "But Mayor Coleman and Bob Naegele both had a lot of courage, stepped up, and found a way to make it work. I did what I could to help them out."

Earlier that decade, Sperling played major roles in getting Coors Field built in Denver and Miller Park in Milwaukee, bringing Major League Baseball to Colorado and keeping it in Wisconsin. After moving around a bit, Sperling would set down some roots in Minnesota, assisting Naegele and his team in getting what would become the Wild off and running.

Not being a hockey guy, Sperling had a unique perspective into how intimate the relationship was between the state and hockey.

After a season-ticket drive yielded incredible results—an honest concern, considering the team's St. Paul location and the fact the North Stars had struggled for years to fill the Met Center—Sperling remembered sending out a mailer to its new ticket buyers.

One of the questions the team wanted to know was how many fans still played the sport. "We got them back, and it was something like 40 percent still played hockey," Sperling said. "Nobody else paid any attention to it, and I was the only non-hockey guy in the room, and I'm saying, 'Holy s***, 40 percent?' How many Vikings fans still play football or Twins fans play baseball? That's a significant number."

That one question made Sperling's job of marketing and selling the team much easier. If it was wondering where its most passionate and supportive fans were, he now had an answer. "They were at the rinks," Sperling said. "There became sort of a genuineness to it, the hockey experience and genuine hockey. And what we were doing appealed to those people, and they knew we were trying to do the right thing."

That authenticity is a trait that still plays a big part in the Wild's brand even today. Inside Xcel Energy Center are hundreds of high school jerseys on the walls, and there is a section honoring youth hockey state champions and several museum areas paying homage to historical figures in the game.

Its most recent "This is Our Ice" campaign began in 2017, where fans bring water from their own lakes and ponds to the arena, where it is used to make the playing surface in the arena. That has its roots back in the days when Sperling, as well as Naegele, team president Matt Majka, and many others branded an organization that has a stake in hockey at all levels throughout the state.

"At the time, I was interested in making this business a success," Sperling said. "Bob believed in me, and I believed in these guys. And the great thing was I didn't get in Doug [Risebrough's] way because I didn't know anything about hockey. All I cared about was basically that we would hit the budget and we'd have a team that would be respectable. And with Jacques Lemaire as coach, that became kind of easy.

"I didn't get caught up in the fan part of it. I tried to keep it balanced with the on-ice performance of an expansion team with the box office and sponsorships and brand."

Sperling spent the better part of 10 years in Minnesota, including time as a minority owner in the club and as chief executive officer of the team. He represented Naegele when he sold the team to Sperling's friend and current Wild owner Craig Leipold.

In the dozens of sports ventures he's participated in over his three decades in the business, Sperling said his time in Minnesota ranks as some of the most rewarding. "It's special, it's really special," Sperling said. "It's special because of what we were trying to do, and I think the emotion we brought to it. It's still there. Some of the other things I've done have been really interesting, and almost everything I've done has been more than just a team; it's trying to be involved in the dynamics of a city and a community. And Minnesota was right there. It's still very special, and I'll never forget it."

93 The Familiar Voice to Minnesota Hockey Fans

If you've ever listened to talk radio in the Twin Cities, whether as a resident or just passing through, chances are you've heard the "familiar voice of Minnesota hockey fans."

Wild television voice Mike Greenlay did color commentary for the team for nearly two decades, but it's his catchy commercials for a local hair transplant website that has earned him plenty of notoriety in recent years.

Greenlay, a Calgary native who reached the NHL as a goaltender during the heyday of the Edmonton Oilers in the late 1980s and had a brief cup of coffee in the national league, has been in the broadcast game since his playing career ended.

During the latter portion of that career, which included stops in Louisville of the ECHL, Atlanta of the IHL, and Hershey of the AHL, the newly married Greenlay was beginning to wonder if he was sick of the grind. He hadn't played in the NHL since the 1989–90 season. As he was getting closer to 30 with a new family to worry about, Greenlay decided to hang up his skates and give broadcasting a try, thanks to friend and broadcaster John Ahlers.

Ahlers met Greenlay when the two were in Louisville at the same time. Now the television voice of the Anaheim Ducks, Ahlers told Greenlay of openings in Detroit and Houston of the IHL to get his broadcasting career going. His parents had just moved to Houston, so he applied and got the job.

Greenlay worked there for one year and spent the next four years traversing the country, working for the Orlando Solar Bears and the Nashville Predators as well as numerous other college and minor league teams. Once he worked five games in five nights for three different leagues in five different cities.

In 1999 Greenlay was named the radio color analyst for the Mighty Ducks of Anaheim, a position he held for two years until he was laid off. Out of hockey and with no jobs available, Greenlay and his wife—now with a two-year-old daughter in tow, moved to Seattle, where he figured he would finish his college education and get a job out of the game. He spent a year there before fate again intervened.

He interviewed for the Wild radio analyst job in 2000 and finished as a finalist, and the job of television analyst was now open. During the summer of 2002, Greenlay tried once more to get back into hockey, sending examples of his work to Minnesota.

This time he got the job. And after moving up and down radio dials for nearly a decade, Greenlay hasn't left broadcasting since.

The Wild has went through a number of television play-by-play voices through the years, starting with Mike Goldberg, now famous for his work with Ultimate Fighting Championships. After him it was Matt McConnell and Dan Terhaar before the team settled on current voice Anthony LaPanta.

Greenlay has sat beside each of those announcers, carving out his own niche and earning his nickname as the "familiar voice of Minnesota hockey fans."

94 Watch a Game in Bemidji

The home of Minnesota's unofficial state holiday, "Hockey Day Minnesota," in 2019, Bemidji is an often forgotten hockey town but a great choice if you are heading north and want to check out a game.

Because it doesn't have the high school success of a Roseau or a Warroad, the collegiate success of a Duluth, or the presence of a museum like Eveleth, the city on the shores of Lake Bemidji carries with it a quiet confidence when it comes to its own hockey history.

When it comes to collegiate success, at least when compared to the University of Minnesota Duluth, perhaps there should be a qualifier: Division I success. Short of a miracle run to the NCAA Frozen Four in 2009, the Bemidji State University Beavers have not come close to winning an NCAA Division I national championship. But the school has had championship seasons.

On the contrary, Bemidji State won four NAIA national championships during the 1970s, a Division II and a Division III championship in the 1980s, and four Division II national championships in the 1990s before becoming a Division I team full time for the 1999–2000 season, joining the College Hockey America conference.

Between 1993 and 1998, the Beavers reached the NCAA Division II championship game six consecutive seasons, winning four titles.

BSU won the CHA playoff championship four times between 2000 and 2010, playing in four NCAA tournaments. Its 2009 run was its most memorable at the D-I level, as Bemidji State leveled Notre Dame 5–1 in the opening round of the tournament that season. The Fighting Irish entered the NCAAs that year as the second-ranked team in the country.

In the region final, the Beavers scored another upset, winning 4–1 against Cornell to advance to the Frozen Four in Washington DC. BSU's Cinderella run came to an end in the national semifinals, as the Beavers lost 4–1 to Miami of Ohio.

Despite its history and its championships, BSU was on the brink of elimination if it couldn't find a way to get into the Western Collegiate Hockey Association. The CHA was dying, and travel was becoming too expensive. But to get into the WCHA, which had much easier travel and several regional rivals, the school and the city of Bemidji would need to build a new arena to replace the antiquated John Glas Fieldhouse.

The result was the Bemidji Regional Events Center, later renamed the Sanford Center. The building, located across Lake Bemidji from downtown, seats about 4,500 fans for hockey and is one of the finest buildings in the state to watch a game in.

Come in the wintertime and you can stay downtown and ride a snowmobile across the lake to the arena or park in one of the many spacious lots outside the building.

When you're in town, check out the Bemidji Curling Club, whose teams have won more than 50 state and national championships.

There are plenty of chain restaurants on the northwest reaches of town, but the real secrets are downtown, where the local shops are. The Minnesota Nice Café is a fantastic place to get breakfast and is right next door to the historic Bemidji Woolen Mills, where you can pick up all of your local knickknacks. Bar 209 has a menu of unique hamburger options. Try the Mac and Cheese Burger; you won't regret it.

95 Neal Broten

A native of Roseau, Neal Broten grew up and came of age in front of hockey fans in his home state. Born November 29, 1959, Broten first found superstardom as a member of the Roseau High School team that went to multiple state tournaments. The Rams never won the championship with Roseau, but his appearances in the Twin Cities were the first of many over the years.

"That was one of the most disappointing things. I can remember coming home when I was a senior on the bus. Your senior year is done; you're done playing with all your buddies. The emotions started. Once you got five miles from town, you could see the water tower, things kind of hit you," Broten told ESPN in 2014. "I knew I was going to the University of Minnesota, but still I'm not going to play with these guys ever again. I grew up playing with them for 10 years. It was an emotional time. I did tear up a little bit driving on that school bus, thinking, *Man, this is it.*"

As a freshman for the University of Minnesota in 1979, Broten scored the game-winning goal in the national championship game, a goal that gave the Golden Gophers their third title during the 1970s. The goal came against rival North Dakota; Broten cruised into the offensive zone down the left-wing side, absorbing a body check and poking the puck into the goal while falling to the ice. To this day, Broten's goal is one of the most iconic ever scored at the University of Minnesota.

The following season, Broten took his talents to the national level, joining several teammates as well as his coach with the Gophers, Herb Brooks, on the U.S. Olympic team. Broten was one of the team's linchpins as the United States won gold for the first time in 20 years as a part of the fabled "Miracle on Ice."

Broten would return for one more season at the University of Minnesota, securing All-American honors as a sophomore in 1981 and helping lead the Gophers back to the national championship game. He also won the first-ever Hobey Baker Award that season as college hockey's top player.

With little left to prove as an amateur, Broten turned professional and signed with the Minnesota North Stars, who had drafted him in the second round of the 1979 NHL Entry Draft.

In his first full season in the NHL, Broten scored 38 goals and had 98 points in 73 games, immediately establishing himself as one of the top young players in the league. He would go on to post 80-plus points in a season three more times in his career, including 1985–86, when he scored 29 goals and posted 105 points, becoming the first American-born player to reach the century mark in points in a single season.

While his point-scoring prowess was well known, Broten was also a part of some unique history; he was Wayne Gretzky's opponent in the Great One's only fight in the NHL in 1982.

Broten was a part of two conference champion North Star teams, reaching the Stanley Cup Finals twice, but he was never able to bring the fabled trophy to his home state. He departed with the team when it moved to Dallas in 1993 and played a season and a half for the Stars in Texas before a trade to the New Jersey Devils gave him a chance at the Cup.

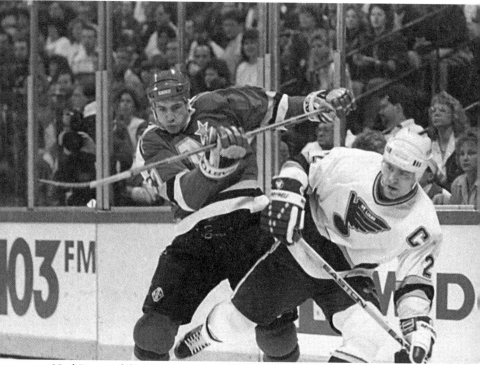

Neal Broten of the Minnesota North Stars checks St. Louis Blues defender Scott Stevens during the first period of a 1991 playoff game.

During the 1995 playoffs, Broten scored seven goals—including four game winners—leading New Jersey to the championship. In doing so, he became the first Golden Gopher to have his name inscribed on the trophy.

Broten wrapped up his career with New Jersey, Los Angeles, and Dallas during the 1996–97 season, retiring to his farm in Wisconsin to live a quiet life in relative anonymity. But to hockey fans in Minnesota, Broten was anything but invisible. He carries a legacy unlike any other player to hail from the state, finishing his career with a national championship, a Hobey Baker Award, an Olympic gold medal, and a Stanley Cup.

"He kind of helped make Minnesota high school hockey well known and created a rich tradition of good players coming out of there," St. Paul native and Tampa Bay Lightning defenseman Ryan McDonagh told ESPN. "He's definitely a big name and done lots for the game in Minnesota. Everybody just remembered how much he would win and how much he would do for his team. It seemed like he would always put his team on his shoulders and help them win."

In 2000 Broten was inducted into the U.S. Hockey Hall of Fame in Eveleth. "He's one of the greatest players the state has ever had. He played with the attitude of a kid playing pond hockey. You just have fun at it," former North Stars general manager Lou Nanne told ESPN. "That's the way he approached it, and that's the way he played. He played with a great amount of skill. He was a tremendous hockey player."

96 "Let's Go Crazy!"

For more than a decade, the Wild used Joe Satriani's "Crowd Chant" following a goal and the ensuing horn. The song was one that certainly got plenty of crowd participation, but it was also not unique, even to the NHL. The New York Islanders also used the Satriani hit following their goals.

It took the death of a Minnesota music icon for the Wild to toy with the idea of using something else.

Once Prince passed suddenly in April of 2016, the Wild decided to honor the legend by temporarily changing the team's goal song to "Let's Go Crazy!" for its Game 6 first-round playoff game against the Dallas Stars.

Center Jordan Schroeder scores on Dallas Stars goalie Antti Niemi during the first period of a 2016 playoff game.

For two periods, the Wild never even got to take the new song for a spin. Facing elimination, Minnesota trailed 4–0 after 40 minutes and appeared destined to go meekly into yet another off-season.

Suddenly, the Wild came alive.

Jared Spurgeon scored 3:48 into the third period as Prince's hit filled the Xcel Energy Center for the first time.

It didn't take long for a repeat performance. Just 16 seconds passed before Jonas Brodin's shot eluded Stars goaltender Kari Lehtonen. The horn and the song just about blew the top off Xcel Energy Center, forcing Dallas to call its timeout to try and slow the momentum.

Four minutes after Brodin cut the lead in half, Spurgeon scored his second of the game off a fantastic backhand pass by Mikko Koivu. Suddenly, Dallas' insurmountable four-goal lead was shaved to just one with more than 11 minutes to play.

Alex Goligoski quieted the building with a goal to make it 5–3 less than two minutes later, but Jason Pominville made it 5–4 with just under five minutes to play.

The Wild made a giant push in the final minute as well, appearing to tie the score with seconds remaining on what would have been a Charlie Coyle goal. Some replay angles seemed to show the puck behind the goal line, but none of them were the all-important overhead camera.

Minnesota's rally fell short, and its season ended that after-noon, but the fan experience in the third period that day stuck with many in attendance. What had already been a quiet push by some to change the goal song became a roar.

That summer the team sent out a survey to season-ticket holders asking for their opinion. They voted by nearly a two-to-one margin to stick with the local legend permanently, a change that lasted two seasons. Eventually tradition became too important to ignore, and "Crowd Chant" was reinstalled as goal anthem before the 2018–19 season.

97 Pierre-Marc Bouchard

Before the Wild had Mikael Granlund dishing out ridiculous assists, it had arguably the most creative player in franchise history doing the same.

Drafted eighth overall by the Wild in the 2002 NHL Entry Draft, Pierre-Marc Bouchard followed Marian Gaborik and Mikko Koivu as the first two first-round draft picks in franchise history. Often forgotten is the quality of career Bouchard had in a Wild uniform despite his diminutive stature and a career filled with unfortunate injuries.

A prodigious scorer in the Quebec Major Junior Hockey League, Bouchard scored 46 goals and 94 assists in just 69 games during his final season in the league with Chicoutimi the year before he was drafted. That season still ranks as one of the all-time great offensive campaigns in league history.

Following the draft, Bouchard was an immediate entrant into the Wild's lineup as an 18-year-old. In retrospect, his debut probably came too early. Listed at 5'10" and just a shade under 170 pounds (late in his career), Bouchard was much smaller and lighter than nearly everyone he played against.

That didn't slow him from scoring seven goals and 20 points in 50 games that season, the year the Wild advanced to the Western Conference Finals. Amazingly, Bouchard played in just five games during that playoff run, assisting on one goal.

Bouchard played in 61 games the following year, then spent the lockout year of 2004–05 in Houston, where he scored 54 points in 67 games with the Aeros. The AHL was a much better league that season, as a number of NHL players played in it because of the lockout.

His breakout year in the AHL was a sign of things to come. Bouchard would score 17 goals and 59 points in 80 games in the year after the lockout and play in all 82 games, scoring 20 goals and 57 points in 2006–07.

He tallied a career best 63 points in 2007–08 before his career fell off a cliff—and not for reasons he could control. Still just 24 years old, Bouchard wasn't even entering the prime of his career in 2008–09. He played in 71 games that season, scoring 46 points, but it was what happened in the 71st game that changed the course of his career forever.

Digging out a puck in the left corner in the defensive zone, New York Islanders forward Nate Thompson blasted Bouchard with a clean hit that knocked Bouchard in the air and head first off the glass and boards. Slow to the bench, Bouchard didn't play another game that season after being diagnosed with a concussion.

The following year, Bouchard played in the season opener against Columbus, hopping over the boards for 14 shifts and nearly 11 minutes in ice time. It was his only action of the season. Concussion symptoms reappeared, and Bouchard was shut down for more than a year.

He returned 14 months later on December 1, 2010, scoring one goal and dishing out three assists in his first five games back from the injury. He showed little rust, scoring 38 points in 59 games his first season back.

Unfortunately for Bouchard and the Wild, his concussion problems were not over. In Winnipeg on December 13, 2011, he took a nasty cross-check from Jets defenseman Zach Bogosian, going head and mouth first into the dasher boards behind the Wild goal. Minnesota was the best team in the NHL at the time, and Bouchard's 18 points in 29 games were a big reason why. The Wild were 20–7–2 in games Bouchard had played in up until that point.

Bouchard played just eight more games that season, taking another shot to the head less than a month later in Vancouver, a hit that ended his season for good.

His final season with Minnesota came in the lockout-shortened season of 2012–13, when he played in 43 of 48 games and scored eight goals and 20 points. Bouchard became a free agent after that season, and with the team close to the salary cap, the Wild couldn't afford to take the risk of signing him. He went on to play one season with the Islanders and another two years in Switzerland, where he won a league MVP award, before retiring from pro hockey in 2016.

Bouchard was one of the most skilled players to ever wear a Wild uniform, and one can only wonder how different his career may have been had he not sustained the concussion in 2009.

98 TRIA Rink

From the early days of Craig Leipold's time as owner of the Wild, one of his top priorities was a state-of-the-art practice facility for the Wild in downtown St. Paul.

Finally, in 2018, Leipold got his wish with the brand new TRIA Rink opening its doors. About four blocks from Xcel Energy Center, the facility—located in what used to be a Dayton's Department Store—became a one-of-a-kind building. Perhaps most prominent, the ice sheet itself is on the highest floor of the six-story building, overlooking downtown St. Paul through a wall of glass windows to the north.

The floors below the rink feature shopping, coffee shops, office space, a tap room, and more, and on the bottom floor, the Wild have their locker room and team gathering spaces.

Shuttling players from the dressing room to the practice rink is an elevator used exclusively by the team when it's in the building, meaning the walk from the locker stall to the ice sheet is no longer than it would be if the team were practicing at Xcel Energy Center.

"Finally having a home is a huge benefit," said Jamie Spencer, Wild executive vice president of business development. "All the strength and training programs we'll be able to do, all the rehab we'll be able to accomplish with the therapy tubs and HydroWorx pools, and the addition of the theater room for video work. Five to 10 years ago, we didn't have video coaches, and now that's become vital to understanding the teams you're playing. The game has changed a lot."

And Spencer would know. A former standout hockey player at the University of Wisconsin, Spencer spearheaded the Wild's efforts to build the practice rink ever since he returned to the club following a stint with the Tampa Bay Lightning.

Xcel Energy Center is one of the finest home ice advantages in the NHL, but it's also home to dozens of concerts, trade shows, and other events that keep the building packed year round.

The Wild plays 41 home games during the regular season, two or three more in the preseason, and potentially several more during the playoffs, and the building is forced to schedule those other events around its anchor tenant's game schedule. That has often made things difficult for practices. In recent years, the Wild has gone to several area rinks for occasional practices while Xcel Energy Center was being used. Now with TRIA Rink, it has a permanent practice home. That means no more dress-and-drive practices and no more shuttling equipment to and from the arena to cramped quarters in the suburbs.

TRIA has its own equipment and own gathering places that serves as a second home for Wild players and staff. The only time the team is expected to be at Xcel Energy Center will now be on gamedays.

The team also plans to use TRIA Rink as a highlight of its recruiting pitches to potential college and professional free agents.

In addition, the facility will serve as the home rink for the National Women's Hockey League's Minnesota Whitecaps and both of Hamline University's hockey teams as well as the home base for area youth hockey teams. "It's more than a practice facility; it's more than a rink for the Wild," Spencer said. "It will truly be hockey for everyone."

99 Women's Pro Hockey Comes to Town

When the National Women's Hockey League was formed in 2015, there was one notable omission from the first four teams. Although the league was based in the northeastern United States and the Founding Four were each within a few hours' drive of each other, the lack of a team in Minnesota seemed like an oversight.

The Boston Pride, Buffalo Beauts, Connecticut Whale, and New York Riveters were the core four of the NWHL, helping to establish the league and get it off the ground.

In the spring of 2018, however, Minnesota finally gained its rightful place in the NWHL when it was announced the Minnesota Whitecaps would join the league for the 2018–19 season. It seemed like it was only a matter of time.

Some of the best women's hockey teams in the country have come from Minnesota, and many of its best players also hailed from the State of Hockey. Each of the first five NCAA championship teams were in-state clubs, including the UMD Bulldogs and University of Minnesota Golden Gophers, who combined to win 11 championships between 2001 and 2019. During that stretch, four schools have won national titles, and half of those came from Minnesota.

The University of Wisconsin, which won five titles during that time, had several players from the state of Minnesota contributing.

Seven members of the 2018 U.S. Olympic women's hockey team that won gold in South Korea were Minnesota natives, more than any other state represented on the team.

Women's hockey in the state also made history in August of 2018 when Eagan native Natalie Darwitz became the fifth female—but first Minnesotan—named to the U.S. Hockey Hall of Fame in Eveleth.

For years, the Whitecaps played an independent schedule, mostly against area college teams. The Whitecaps themselves were filled with players who had graduated from college but had few options in terms of playing the sport competitively beyond those years.

Members of the Western Women's Hockey League before that, a league that folded in 2011 because of financial difficulties, the Whitecaps rejoined the professional ranks on May 15, 2018, when they were announced as the newest members of the NWHL. Playing their games at TRIA Rink, the practice facility of the Minnesota Wild, the Whitecaps began play in the fall of 2018 as the newest pro team in the state and it didn't take long for them to make their mark. The Whitecaps won the Isobel Cup as NWHL champions in their first season in the league.

100 Wooger

One of many branches of the John Mariucci coaching tree, Doug Woog became one of the most successful collegiate head coaches in the country while guiding the University of Minnesota men's hockey team for a decade and a half.

A native of South St. Paul, Woog was a three-time All-State player in high school, leading the Packers to four consecutive state tournament berths. It was his first of two successful stints at the school, his second coming as a coach more than a decade later.

In between, Woog played three years for Mariucci with the Golden Gophers, where as a junior in 1965, Woog was named an All-American. He was the team's Most Valuable Player as a senior before graduating with a degree in education in 1967. His diploma would come in handy over the next three decades, as Woog transitioned to a new role behind the bench.

Woog coached six years at the junior hockey level beginning in 1971, first with the Minnesota Junior Stars, a team that later became the St. Paul Vulcans. In his first venture into coaching, Woog served as an assistant under his former teammate with the Gophers, Herb Brooks, who was head coach of the Junior Stars.

After becoming a head coach in 1973, Woog won a pair of U.S. Junior National Championships. In 1977 Woog returned to the Packers as the head coach of the boys' team. In six years with South St. Paul, Woog's teams advanced to the state tournament four times and won two conference championships.

Woog moved on to the U.S. national ranks in the early 1980s, serving in a number of roles, including as an assistant for the United States Olympic Team in 1984. It was an experience that helped launch him into the role he's best known for in the State of Hockey: a 14-year tenure as head coach at his alma mater at the U of M.

Woog did everything but win a national championship with the Gophers, reaching the NCAA tournament in each of his first 12 seasons as head coach. Six times, including in each of his first four seasons, the Gophers reached the Frozen Four, finishing fourth once, third twice, and in arguably his most crushing defeat, a runner-up finish in 1989.

Minnesota was playing in the championship game against Harvard at the St. Paul Civic Center minutes from Woog's hometown. Tied 3–3 in overtime, the Gophers' Randy Skarda had the winning goal on his stick but ripped a shot off the nearside post. A goal would have given Minnesota its fourth national championship and snapped a 10-year drought for what was one of college hockey's most dominant programs.

Instead, Harvard would win the game minutes later on a goal by Ed Krayer.

Minnesota would reach two more Frozen Fours during the next six years but would never come as close to winning a championship under Woog as it did in 1989.

In 14 years Woog had two losing seasons with the Gophers—his final two campaigns—and the coach resigned following the 1998–99 season, when he was replaced by Don Lucia. At the time of his retirement from coaching, Woog was the program's all-time winningest coach, posting a 389–187–40 record.

Woog transitioned to an assistant athletic director role and into television, where he spent a decade as the Gophers' color commentator on Fox Sports North broadcasts. On TV his quirky personality showed through, and he developed a bit of a cult following thanks to his unique descriptions and metaphors.

In 2015 the city of South St. Paul renamed its hockey facility, then known as Wakota Arena, as Doug Woog Arena. The building, which opened the same year Woog graduated from South St. Paul High School, houses two rinks, six locker rooms, an off-ice training area, community space, and warm areas to watch games from. It is located off Concord Boulevard, one block north of Interstate 494 in South St. Paul.

Acknowledgments

The phrase "Minnesota Nice" certainly applies when thinking about who to thank when it comes to assistance in writing this book. I've personally lived and witnessed much of the "modern" era of the Wild in that I've been able to write so much about the second decade of the franchise.

But learning about the first era of the club was a truly fascinating adventure.

The willingness of former players like Wes Walz, Andrew Brunette, and Dwayne Roloson to share their stories is truly appreciated.

I could have asked Doug Risebrough a million questions about how he wanted to build the club and his vision for bringing a Stanley Cup to Minnesota.

Matt Majka has seen it all, and without his support and that of the organization—not only allowing me the freedom to pursue this project, but also to encourage me to do it well—I wouldn't have been able to accomplish it.

Bob Naegele really was as nice a man as everyone says he was. I'm so lucky to have been able to discuss the Wild for this book before he passed away in 2018. Roger Godin is a walking, talking hockey museum. The city of Eveleth, Minnesota, is magical.

Norm Coleman and Jac Sperling aren't native Minnesotans, but their steadfast pursuit of professional hockey is one every Wild fan should be thankful for.

A special thanks to Shane Frederick for showing me how to be a hockey writer, as well as the support and friendly competition from my colleagues past, present, and future. You make me better every day.

To the hundreds of players, coaches, and executives over the years who have allowed me to tell their stories, as well as the folks out there who read them, share them, or even criticize them, I say thank you.

My mom and dad have been my No. 1 fans my entire life. Making you proud is a goal I shoot for on a daily basis. Hopefully, I achieve it at least every once in a while.

And last, but certainly not least, so much credit for this book goes to my wife, Jen, who spent two years as a hockey widow. Between travelling to cover the Wild and spending hour upon hour reading and writing about the Wild, I've been a ghost. I could not have finished this without your unwavering love and support.

Sources

Books

Godin, Roger. *Before the Stars: Early Major League Hockey and the St. Paul Athletic Club Team*; Minnesota Historical Society Press (2005).

Godin, Roger. *Red, White and Blue on Ice: Minnesota's Elite Teams and Players of the 1920s, 30s and 40s*; Saint Johann Press (2010).

Lynn, Tom. *How to Bake an NHL Franchise from Scratch: The First Era of the Minnesota Wild*; CreateSpace Independent Publishing Platform (2014).

Bernstein, Ross. *Wearing the "C": Leadership Secrets from Hockey's Greatest Captains*; Triumph Books (2012).

Newspapers

Minneapolis Star Tribune
St. Paul Pioneer Press
Duluth News Tribune
The Fargo Forum

Personal Interviews

Wes Walz	Chuck Fletcher	Jamie Spencer
Bob Naegele	Bruce Boudreau	Bill Robertson
Andrew Brunette	Doug Risebrough	Steve Aronson
Dwayne Roloson	Matt Majka	Mike Greenlay
Ryan Suter	Jac Sperling	Tom Reid
Devan Dubnyk	Roger Godin	Norm Coleman
Matt Cullen	Michael Russo	Arne Carlson
Mike Yeo	Glen Andresen	

Websites
Hockey-reference.com
ESPN.com
NHL.com
NHL.com/Wild
NYTimes.com
DMagazine.com
SI.com
Minnesotahockey.org
Minnesotahockeymag.org
History.vintagemnhockey.com
Sportsbusinessdaily.com
ThePlayersTribune.com

Miscellaneous
The United States Hockey Hall of Fame and Museum
Minnesota Wild media guide
Hamline University Athletics
NHL Guide and Record Book